Bestsellers and Badsellers

Bestsellers and Badsellers

Towards other strategies for publishing books: the Dutch case

HERMANN BUSS

Copyright Hermann Buss, 2015

DESSET PUBLISHERS

BESTSELLERS and BADSELLERS

Towards other strategies for publishing books: the Dutch case

Copyright 2016 Hermann Buss

All Rights Reserved

Cover design: Hans Ringnalda

Contact: bestbadsellers@gmail.com

More info: http://www.bestbadsellers.com

Published in the Netherlands by Desset Publishers

ISBN 978-1523690077

Version 1 EN

[Why this book]

'A change always triggers the next one.'

Niccolo Machiavelli

The market for books in the Netherlands shrank over the past five years with at least 25%. And as far as we can see growth is nowhere near in sight. For publishers, authors and new entrepreneurs this is not a fine outlook.

This book helps to gain insight in the current business of publishing books, a typical business where overproduction or 'waste' is paramount.

But foremost this book wants to form a basis for developing new ways of publishing. Sometimes it seems as if publishers are forced to create only bestsellers, but in the process of publishing this book gives him a way out to - profitably- excercise his role in bookpublishing in a healthy and succesful way. This book puts forward improvements on the one hand, and proves on the other hand that there are other viable businessmodels for publishing. Based on a benchmark of 14 Dutch publishers not only three new publisher types were developed, but also strategies to improve and develop every type of publisher to a higher professional level.

[Contents]

'When I was tired of searching, I discovered the art of finding.'

Friedrich Nietzsche

[Introduction]

'What is asserted without proof can be denied without proof.'

Euclid

The daily practice of book publishing shows serious signs of wear and tear. The market for books in the Netherlands has declined in recent years by 2 to 5% per year and this trend seems to be continuing. Not only in the Netherlands, this decline is visible; there is a shrinking global trend that puts the once vibrant and thriving industry under severe pressure.

Speculating on the reasons has been a nice pastime. Some argue that the decline is related to the fact that more people read less and less due to the poorer reading instruction of youth and young adults. Others blame it on the crisis. Still others say it is due to the rise of the Internet and alternative means of entertainment. On all such speculation and defeatism this book does not contribute: I'd rather stick to the facts.

What is a book anyway?

A book is equivalent to a 'narrative experience through reading.' This definition is important when we talk about books. A book - let's be clear - is but one embodiment of the narrative experience. Since man exists, he tried his stories and messages to convey through speech or through the writing on clay tablets, papyri and rocks.

Only when it became important to produce copies from the story, copyists emerged (in Roman and medieval times), culminating in the invention of the printing press in the Middle Ages.

By this latter invention it was suddenly possible to produce a 'scalable' story, ie. from a single story infinitely many copies could be made without significant 'scaling up' of resources. (Example: to make as many copies of books they needed a proportional number of writers or scribes, with the printing press only a single printing machine was required)

But a movie, a video, a story that's read, a paper book, a PDF, an app and so on, are also embodiments of the narrative experience.

I'll be the first to agree that the experience through reading is different from the other implementation like a movie and that it requires very different 'skill sets' from producers and performers.

This book is not about the other narrative forms and how they are produced; I focus specifically on the narrative experience of the book, and hence the paper versions of the story (P-book) and its digital version (PDF or E-book). By 'publishing' I mean particularly the consumer-driven publishing industry of fiction and nonfiction.

The professional look at the publishing house

In my daily practice, first as a director of a major publisher and later as a consultant and interim manager of media companies, I noticed that there is little knowledge of operational analysis in this industry. Although there are data on sales and revenues, the data are not structurally used. Rather, there is information (eg in the form of monthly reports, pre - and post calculations and budgets), but that information is hardly used for analysis or innovation purposes.

In an industry that is mainly dominated and managed by people who have a strong background in languages and 'humanities' and are mainly 'lingual' oriented, it is not surprising that more beta sciences - oriented, numerical and analytical approaches produce adverse reactions. Especially if these analyses were hitherto not necessary because money flowed abundantly - as in the 80s and 90s of the last century.

The gamma function in the industry, marketing, analysis and brand positions within the publishing houses is all put at the end of the process and often dismissed as marketing communication or promotion. Illustrative of this is the book *Merchants of Culture* by John B. Thompson (2010), in which the author (a professor of sociology) needs 400 closely written pages to describe the British and American book publishing industry. It is true that he used a number of tables, but he describes the publishing market with minimal financial analysis.

But in a market where money is not as easily earned as in the 80s and 90s, the weaknesses with publishers show quickly. As said the marketing function is a purely promotional or marketing function: it becomes painfully clear that there is no insight in who the readers are and that there has never been done any structural research in profiles and needs of customers.

Also, it is striking that substantial investments in innovation for new markets and new products never really have been made. And then it's no surprise that Amazon, Bol.com and Apple - just to name a few - are much better positioned to take on this market: they know exactly who the customer is and what his behavior is like; and they invest substantial percentages of their turnover in acquisitions, participations and own innovations. Example: Amazon annually invests 6% of its turnover in innovative products and services.

But even more striking is that many publishers in the course of time, generate waste at many points in the publishing process chain. This waste creates a disproportionate capital requirement for titles that do basically nothing in the market. The players will say that it has always been that way: the bestsellers always created surplus capital to absorb the bad selling titles. However, the number of books sold are dwindling, making this internal subsidy system fall apart.

The business model of publishers has always depended heavily on the surplus that bestsellers yielded. Balancing the product portfolio of different types of books never really happened. 'Publish Fewer Titles' now seems to be the motto. Cutting costs (because that is what happens if you publish less titles) can be done by everyone, but changing the structure of spending and the way you publish is quite another matter; therefore you have to consciously think about the publishing chain, but also on innovation and the business model.

Strategies

This book aims to answer the question of how to change and improve that structure. I found the answer in three strategies or publisher types as you like. The basis for this strategy I support by first discussing and analysing all cost components of publishers in fiction and nonfiction. To make cogent statements and to establish conditions for the new strategy, I make use of a benchmark that is specifically designed for the Dutch situation. The benchmark is Dutch, but can also be used for non Dutch markets at a later stage.

A difficult point in my research was the access to the financial costs within the publishing process at title level. Few publishers keep to detail the cost of a book. That's why I've modelled certain aspects of costs that are as closely as possible to real life. The results of the survey reflect a conclusion that the whole publishing world has been working on: that investing in small titles demands a much better focus and discipline than hitherto. The amount of capital required is huge when it comes to 'badsellers'. Of course it is attractive to invest in best-sellers, but that advice is too short-sighted.

What I want to make clear in this book is that you can still choose to publish old-style, but that you have to choose a different focus and mission, in other words: a new strategy. I also indicate that the Dutch market still leaves room for bestseller publishers, but that market will not be easy for the smaller publishers to enter, not in the least because of the necessary capital strength and risk management.

That seems to contradict the steadily shrinking of larger publishing houses in the Netherlands and a spin-off trend in 2014 (for example, Weekblad Pers Groep(WPG)); internationally however, there is still a trend towards concentration (Penguin), which is motivated by the same objective of risk and the ability to release large budgets that large companies can handle better - for example in comparison to the film and music industries.

This book's road map

The book *Blockbusters*, from the Dutch media expert and professor at Harvard Business School, Anita Elberse, was my inspiration for research into the properties of the Dutch book industry. The book also was the impetus for the development of my alternative strategy and business model for publishing as we know it. The aforementioned book by Thompson was also an inspiration by his sharp description of how the publishing world works. Research by Viguerie and his co-authors, recorded in the book *Granularity of Growth* forms the basis for the strategic considerations of this book. For readability, I have added the summary of Vigueries theory separately in an Annex.

. In the section *Market* the Dutch market for books is summarized and the specifics are described.

. In the part *Insight* all relevant cost elements of a book are named and discussed.

. In the section *Benchmark* results from the benchmark of 14 publishers are discussed and questions are formulated that serve as the basis for the proposal of new strategies.

. In the part *Strategy* three conditions that must be met are proposed before three resulting strategies are discussed. The relationship between the three strategies will be explained and discussed.

. Everything comes together in the *Test* part as individual publishers are analysed on the basis of the benchmark and it is discussed which strategy is best suited in the relevant cases.

. The *Appendices* contain the summary of the theory of Viguerie and the benchmark elements are presented as well.

Publishers for consumers must reinvent themselves. Hopefully this book helps to achieve that.

[Market]

'Just because publishing is going digital doesn't mean that there's a new road to publishing riches. It's the same tough slog.'

Thad McIlroy

The Dutch market for books amounts to around half a billion Euros. We are talking in this case about 'General books', which are called in the Dutch jargon A-books. The Royal Dutch Society for the Book Trade (KVB) defines the A-book as ' General books - books like novels, thrillers, poetry, children's books and non-fiction books (non-fiction). For the Dutch A-book a fixed book price law exists'.

In practice books being handled by bookstores and distribution channels are classified into A-books, O-books, S and W-books. For the A (general) books, a standard rate of 42% of the selling price, which is actually a mandatory discount is agreed between publisher and bookseller. Special deals can be made to this rule, but the selling price is fixed by law.

The O-books are mainly specialist books. Therefore free rates apply toward the bookstore which are around 25-30% of the selling price (still fixed by law) and where the publisher determines a number of cost components himself.

S (chool) - and W (Science) books also have their own agreements, which are quite different for each channel.

This book actually covers (mainly) A -books.

Chapter1

The Dutch Market for publishing books

The Dutch market for general books has in recent years seen a continuing decline in sales. The narrative experience first consisted solely of P-books and lately also by E-books. But the rise of the E-book does not compensate by far the contraction of paper editions of (mostly) the same stories. You can see that in the figure below.

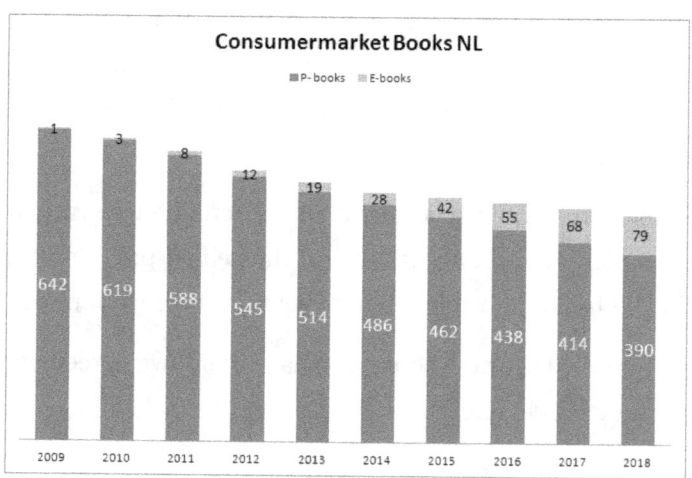

Fig. 1.1 Revenues Dutch Consumermarket Books 2009-2018 (in € million), source: PwC mediaoutlook 2014

The consumer market lost approximately € 130 million in five years. The rate in which the market for P-books shrank in the period from 2009 (which was a record year for the Dutch book trade) until 2014 is almost 25% (!).

The sales volume of E-books was indeed twenty-seven times that in the year 2009, but limited the overall market decline to 20% compared to 2009, and thus threw the market back to the sales level of the late 90s.

Number of titles and distribution

In the Netherlands in 2014 according to figures from the Centraal Boekhuis (a unique joint venture of both publishers and bookstores, that has a single warehouse for all books in the Netherlands and a distribution facility for E-books as well) about 80,000 titles were available in print, provided by 1000 publishers and sold in about 1,700 bookstores. Bookstore sales are estimated at 38 million units in 2014. An interesting detail is that Bol.com since 2013 is the largest retail party for books. In 2014 Amazon entered this market, but Amazon.nl delivers as of writing this book only E-books. E-books are about 36 000 titles (with 291 publishers), which sold approximately 3.3 million copies in 2014 (not including piracy versions), primarily via webshops.

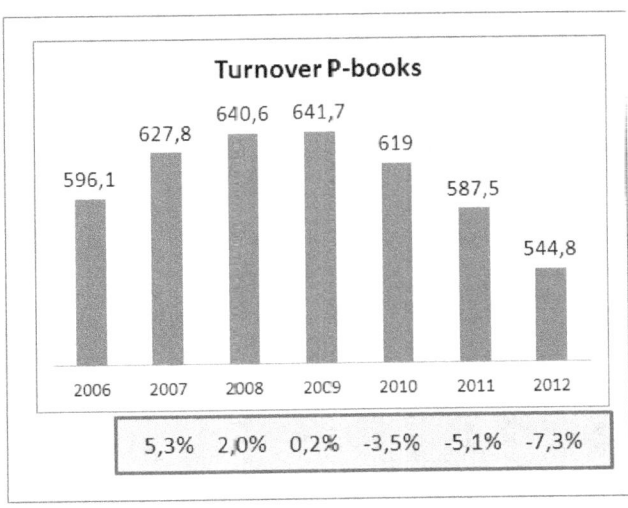

Fig. 1.2 Revenue(in € million) and CAGR growth (in %) of paper A-books in the Netherlands 2006-2012, source GfK

Estimates for the size of piracy are not available but it is generally assumed to be significant and greatly affect the above figures. Consultancy bureau GfK calculated in 2014 that the average e-reader in the Netherlands contains 90% illegal and free content and previews. A Dutch e-reader in 2014 held an average of 117 E-books, of which only 11 are actually paid for according to this estimate.

Not everything is in Dutch

Of the books sold in the Netherlands, the majority is written by foreign authors and often translated into Dutch. Translation costs are therefore an important part of the production costs of books. To be precise: around 30% of the titles sold consists of original Dutch manuscripts, 70% has been translated. For comparison: in England the translated share of the market is a sheer 3%, in Germany 7% and in France 14%.

That is an inherent drawback of a small language like Dutch. Please bear in mind that the Netherlands have 17 million inhabitants as compared to bigger countries like Germany (81 million), The United Kingdom (64 million), France (66 million), Italy (60) or Spain (47 million)

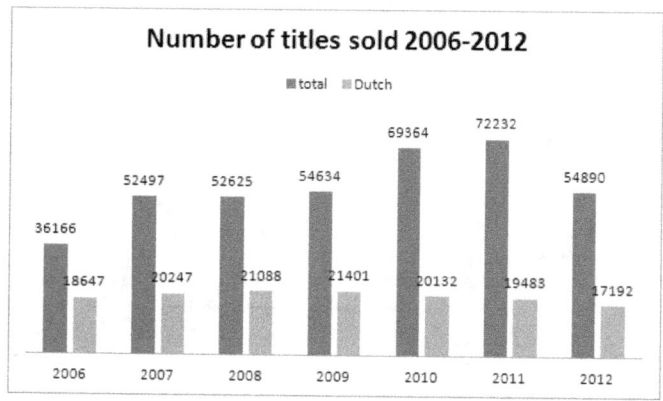

Fig. 1.3 Number of titles of A- books sold in The Netherlands, source KVB

Every year, thousands of new titles appear on the Dutch market. The chart below reflects the number of new appearances of books in any year which are actually on the market. The doubling of the number of new titles from 2006 onwards is primarily due to increased sales of foreign-language titles on the Dutch market.

For comparison reasons, we looked at how many titles as defined by the Royal Library (Koninklijke Bibliotheek, KB) are produced in the Netherlands from 1990 onwards. Each year the Royal Library receives all newly published and reprinted books from most publishers in the Netherlands. Her definition of A-books only differs from that of the KVB: at the KB this includes not only general but all fiction books (original and translated) and non-fiction, as well as scientific publications and monographs. Yet the survey of the KB provides a good indication that the number of titles ended up in 2014 at about the 1990 level.

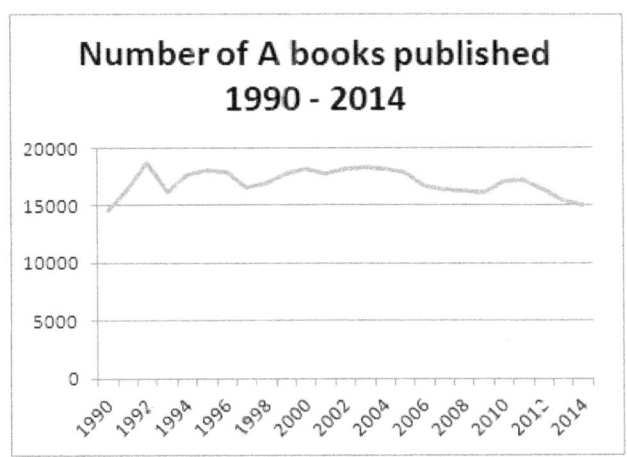

Fig. 1.4 Number of A-books published in 1990-2014, source Koninklijke Bibliotheek

Case 1: Paper is here to stay

With a firm 'print is alive - at least for books' consulting and accounting firm Deloitte did its predictions for the 2015 publishing market. With a lot of research among users, particularly in the USA Deloitte shows that E-books are more than 20% of the turnover of books, but that still 80% will be traded in paper. That's also true for younger readers, the company found out. It is also clear that books are read in striking numbers from mobiles and phablets (combination of smart phone and tablet) and that trend will continue.

The company also believes that the sales of E-books will stabilise at a level of 20-25% of the market, based on US market developments. Striking: in the USA book sales went up by 8% in the same period that the market in the Netherlands shrank by 20-25%!

Case 2: Why is venture capital not willing to invest in (book) publishers?

Is the publishing industry such a fine place to invest in and why does innovation lag behind most of the time? In a presentation (available on Slideshare) Thad McIlroy in 2014 gives us a glimpse into how the publishing industry is perceived by the tough financial world of venture capital and investors. His analysis boils down to the conclusion that digitization has not yet led to very good concepts for the publishing industry that investors consider 'hot'. He gives clear examples that book publishing in any case is not on the radar of investors.

In addition, the publishing sector is an industry that is dominated by Amazon in the eyes of investors; they think it makes little sense to compete with them. McIlroy finds it rather ironic that there are indeed large acquisitions, but in his words, 'big old companies that buy other big old companies', while referring to publishers who take over other publishers.

If the two or three major investments and acquisitions of new concepts are excluded (in the period where McIlroy is talking about there was, among other things, the acquisition of Goodreads by Amazon) then the only risk investment at the time did not exceed $ 35,000 to $ 70,000 - and that's no more than a year's salary for an employee! Not very significant. Venture capital always wants to have a big exit or a high yield. The latter seems not possible in the current investment climate.

Slightly more positive, but no less critical the Spanish agency Dosdoce asks itself in a report the question why publishers aren't more active in partnerships, investments and acquisitions of start-ups. Their investigation leads to surprising insights, for example, that both start-ups and publishers do want to work together but that cooperation has suffered from a lack of knowledge about each other; they do meet each other but often do not to speak each other's language. In addition to that start-ups usually like to make a quick deal and the publishers actually want to stay merely informed about new developments.

From my own experience I add that most start-ups often come along for content (and not always with a clear solution to a problem or opportunity), where the publishers in turn are again reluctant to give that content.

The lack of good innovation contact points within publishing is a huge dissatisfier for collaboration. This was proven in the program *Publisher of the Future* (Uitgeverij van de Toekomst) that ran for several years in the Netherlands, wherein more than 100 publishers participated. The condition was that for this program several publishing houses had to collaborate in innovative projects. Only through an enormous effort by the supervisors could these collaborations take place as the responsible people within the publishers often did innovation 'on the side' of their regluar jobs. Moreover the innovation responsibilities regularly shifted between people within the publisher, therewith innovation being not the most wanted activity in this industry.

The most striking findings of the report of Dosdoce come down to a mismatch between the supply of start-ups and the demand of the publishers:

. The start-ups offer value added services especially in the field of visibility of books and alternative marketing methods, where publishers initially ask for (technical) solutions for online distribution.

. The question is whether start-ups aim too high with their solutions or that the publishers are too far behind with their demand. An attitude that is positive relative to investments in partnerships and acquisitions is a requirement but not often encountered with publishers

[Understanding]

"Regret is not enough, insight would have been better."

Marnix Gijsen

In principle making a book is no different than making a car or a biscuit, but there are elements in the production chain that are specific to this industry. This section looks into this process in as much detail as possible. The insight we gain is needed to understand where the biggest expenses are and thereby the largest capital investments in the publishing process. Based on that we can determine what the parameters are for success for a book and we will develop ideas for improvement. In a later chapter I will propose new strategies. The aim now is to decompose, step by step, prices and costs.

The notion of 'story'

For the analysis we see that a single story can be produced in different ways: as a P-book and as an E-book, but also as a film or a play. Without taking the film and stage rights into consideration here, if you want to see the profitability of 'the story', all the costs and revenues of all the presentation methods (be it on paper or online) should be added. This can be problematic, for example, when a story is published by multiple publishers, or when one story has many different versions (paperback, reprint, hardback, luxury paperback, etc.) with all its different costs.

P-books en E-books

The difference between the cost of a P-book and an E-book is simple to determine. At this point, it is important to indicate when and where these differences occur.

I have collected data over a period of eighteen months and built a benchmark that we will discuss in chapter 11 and further. For simplicity and for understanding, I take all the elements that matter in publishing P-books below point by point. E-books I treat separately. The emphasis is still on P-books, partly because the bulk of the turnover and the cost still comes from this 'traditional' form of production.

Chapter 2

The price of a book

The price of a book is the amount the purchaser, user or reader pays for the text he wants to read. Within the publishing industry one speaks of the consumer or retail price. In the Netherlands there is a law on fixed bookprices ('Wet op de vaste boekenprijs'). The consumerprice is determined in the Netherlands by the publisher. The law indicates that that price may not be altered during a certain period. The underlying idea behind the law is on the one hand to protect the vulnerability of Dutch literature by giving publishers leeway to publish less profitable books to be funded by more succesful books and, secondly, to enable a broad network of bookshops to keep up a broad range so everyone has access to books.

In addition, the law offers the publisher a number of options to determine discounted prices for a limited time. After six months, a publisher may change the price of a book, he may lift the fixed price of a book after a year. Discounts and the like should not be given except in the case of book clubs.

E-books are exempted from the fixed book price, like textbooks and secondhand books. So when a book is stopped ('verramsjt' as it is called) or shredded by the publisher the price is free and the seller himself can determine a different price.

Obviously, there are ways to circumvent that legislation, and some practices will be condoned. Thus, for certain sales chains a publisher can produce a special printrun of a particular title e.g. with a different cover, a different ISBN and thus often a different price. It is a way of creating special discounts.

In general all parties stick to this law, also because everyone keeps a close eye on each other. And parties do not shy to protest and sometimes go to court.

Price differentiation is not (yet) taking place

Price differentiation, a normal tool in every market to differentiate a product, is possible in theory, but it seems not a publisher wants to take advantage of this possibility. Moreover, you can't see any distinction on pricelevel between e.g. novice and established authors, where it might just be a distinctive element.

A certain price differentiation actually takes place only on the basis of the representation (and size) of the book. In general, we distinguish - from high to low price: bound book (hard cover), paperback (more expensive variant), paperback (mid-price), paperback and E-book. There are no cheaper E-book variants, or it should be the individual chapters of the book which frequently appear as teasers or samples for free on sites like Amazon and Google Play.

New calculation models

In the Netherlands there are some experiments on a very modest scale with a sort of all-you-can-eat model for E-books, in which for a fixed price one can read a number of titles per month. For example, publisher VBK offers a model for € 2.99 per month where one has 10 titles selected by an editorial staff. The Dutch public libraries are experimenting with a model for E-books, with a € 10 monthly fee for ten titles to be downloaded at ones personal choice. There is currently a choice of some 5,000 titles.

When we look across the border Amazon with Kindle Unlimited offers for $ 9.99 per month up to ten titles. But here by deleting certain titles from your e reader you can select and download a new title (from a total of 700 000!). In this way you basically have infinite choice. The question is when Amazon will also introduce this service in the Netherlands. Other initiatives are primarily American, such as Oyster and Scribd. There are rumours that 'the streaming read' is coming, comparable to Netflix for movies and series and Spotify for music. Dutch publishers WPG and Lannoo have announced this a few years ago but it is still awaited for reportedly because the legal rights issues are complicated. In fact publishers are very hesitant because of fear for canibalisation of their existing market.

In recent scientific literature there has been given proof that this is not the case and recently I published an article about it (in Dutch). But for the moment publishers shy away form the issue.

Whatever the case, slowly but steadily things are changing in book prices and sales propositions.

Standardprices

Although no price agreements can be made between all the parties involved, certain kinds of informal standard prices or price points have emerged, depending on model, shape and size of the book. This often involves 'psychological prices' as € 19.90 or € 15, -. In recent years more of these kinds of standard prices have emerged. Silently most publishers stick to this psychological pricing, but there are many variations.

For a sample of about 3000 titles (P-book) the sales price is divided by the number of pages (figure 2.1). In 2013 for a consumer the value of a story focused typically around 3 to 4 Eurocents per page. A similar methodology for E-book could be a value per kilobyte. It remains interesting to follow how much customers are willing to pay for a story.

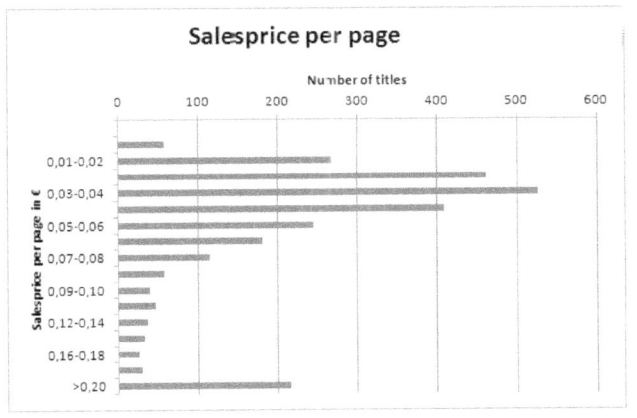

Fig. 2.1 Sample sales price per page of a P-book in 2013

A common explanation is that the prices are relatively high for books in the Netherlands because the language area is small, and therefore printruns are relatively small. Also the fact that many titles are translated in the Netherlands, provides an additional pressure on the price: after all all costs must be divided by a smaller edition, as compared to big issues in countries like Germany or England.

By the phenomenon of self publishing you can also see different price points arise, especially for E-books. Because Amazon is a major player in the field of self-publishing, it is interesting to keep an eye on the development of these prices.

Price regulation varies by country

The Netherlands has no unique model with price regulation (although it is becoming more and more unique because more and more countries drop the fixed book price). Thus France has a similar model, but also the USA has jurisprudence which yields more or less the same effect (for pricing and brand development in USA and UK: see Thompson p299 and further). In the USA the Robinson-Patman Act forbids to suppliers, including publishers, to give various discounts to their distributors. That does not mean there is a fixed book price, but it incurred a fairly open system of price reductions, which made the pricing of books also more or less transparent. Amazon has tried and still tries to break this in - by European standards - hyper agressive ways. For nearly 10 years there is legal hassle between publishers and Amazon, with unclear results so far and hardly any winners

The UK in turn has abandoned the system of discounts - and therefore prices - altogether. The result is sharp price competition in different channels and a cut-throat competition between different retail chains, particularly for bestsellers. It often happens that books are offered below cost (see Thompson for more insights)

Fixed price of books in the Netherlands

There is much debate on fixed book prices, and the end thereof is widely predicted. The consequences of the abolition of the book price will be considerable. We suggest a number of implications:

The sales price will be under pressure due to distribution channels that will want to use the price mechanism to get a better marketposition. There will thus be pressure on the transfer price (which is the price to pay for the sales channel to the publisher) because the sales channels have major purchasing power and publishers will be put under a lot pressure by them. In turn, the publishers will drop the right to return (the possibility for booksellers to return unsold books to the publisher). Royalties for authors who are still based on the consumer price drop automatically. It would not surprise me if the royalties will no longer be determined on the basis of the consumer price but on the basis of the real transfer price per distributionchannel. In other words, the whole price building so to speak will be pulled down, everyone in the chain will suffer until the book reaches a realistic price level. What that real price will be stays unclear, and I refer again to the UK market, where the fixed price was once released with all its effects.

Whatever course the abolition of the fixed book price will take, I think one thing is clear: resourcefulness is an important tool to create new opportunities in this situation. And new opportunities there will be!

VAT

VAT in the Netherlands is 6% for p- books and 21% for E-books or online versions of a story.

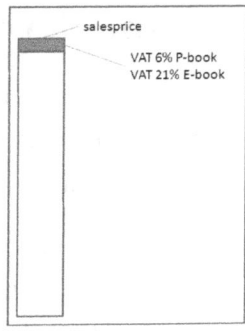

Fig. 2.2 Sales price for P-book and VAT

Sales Channel

The relatively high sales prices are determined by the expensive distribution channel - bookstores and distributors - that require on average 42% of the net selling price in order to exist. Put differently, you could say that the distribution channel has assumed an important position of power. Before the Internet era, there was no alternative for publishers than the bookstore channel to reach customers, with the possible exception of a bookclub such as ECI in the Netherlands.

The huge range of titles from publishers in recent years means that these publishers have become increasingly dependent on sales in the bookstore. As we saw earlier, the title output in 2006 to 2011 in the Netherlands more than doubled (from about 36 000 to around 72 000).

Booksellers themselves operate in a - in theory - relatively risk-free environment, because the bookstores negotiated the 'right to return': unsold books may be returned to the publisher, with a refund of the purchase price.

However many bookstores have had to close, mainly due to lower sales by a general decline in reading, the bankcrisis, high prices and E-book piracy, whereby the capital requirement of the store inventory is relatively high and the turnover rate of capital is too low.

Therefore it sometimes seems bookstores have a less differentiated offer and the shelves seem emptier than before. Smaller stock in the store costs less money, it's that simple. But the major reason for the difficult situation of booksellers is the rise of the online bookstore, in the Netherlands mainly Bol.com, which accounts for about a quarter or more of all book sales.

Online bookstore

Because there is this fixed book price one might expect all publishers would set up large online bookstores (as they often had bookstore chains in possession in the past) to pocket the 42% of the net selling price. Or - if it meant a large share of sales among readers - to have lower consumerprices from the start and therewith giving it back in part to the reader.

But that never took place, partly because Bol.com came into the market and thereby achieved a massive reach among readers in the online channel. In part because of the always dormant channel conflict between publishers and bookstores once publishers would in one way or another move into direct sales. You could also say that publishers have not thought enough about their online presence and the phenomenon of 'online reach'.

Admittedly, most publishers now have a solution to sell books directly: they sell their books through their own site. However, the reach of most of these sites remains too low and is therefore not very relevant. The consumer price therefore remains relatively high.

Building knowledge about customers

But what is more important: what have the publishers and by analogy the authors received from the booksellers in return for that 42% of the net sales price? Sales data is provided, but no data about the customer such as name, address and (online) behavior data such as repeat purchases and the like, with which one can build customer profiles.

This 'new gold of the Internet world' remains with the online retailers like Amazon and Bol.com; bookstores have only POS information and do not know the deeper customer data, either.

Here's the first question that publishers should focus on: what reach do their sales partners have with customers and how can publishers negotiate that they not only get sales (data) but also the customer information?

Other distribution options

We have already talked about other sales methods, such as all-you-can-eat models with VBK and Amazon a.o. There are streaming initiatives, such as Wifi Books, Scribd, and Oyster and there are lending facilities, such as libraries and at Amazon as well. There is also a controversial E-book case in the Netherlands, Tom Kabinet, where people can offer their E-books second hand.

These are all possibilities and ways to allow distribution variants in addition to price. It is driven by the enormous possibilities and penetration of tablets, phablets and smartphones. Here are tremendous growth opportunities for publishers, but the acceptance of such methods is still slow and reluctant.

Transfer price

At this point it is important to note that we can speak of the 'transfer price' of the book after deduction of VAT and distribution channel costs. The transfer price is also known as the wholesale price for the product. In most industries, it is treated as the price over which the supplying company has influence. This observation is important if we are going to look at cost-determining elements such as royalties.

Case: Hachette versus Amazon

An unprecedented fierce battle was waged in the course of 2014 between Amazon and publisher Hachette. The reason was the requirement of Amazon to set the prices for E-books themselves (next to the demand to keep 30%of that price).

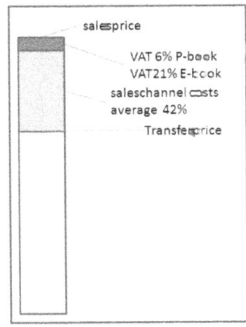

Fig. 2.3. Costs sales channel with respect to purchase price and transfer price

Hachette refused, after which Amazon put all books by Hachette as 'out of stock' on her site. Because Amazon holds approximately 50% of the US book trade, both publishers and authors would suffer from this one sided action. The action of Amazon seemed to explode in her face when hundreds of authors united in a violent protest against the practices of Amazon, in a full-page ad (on paper that is!) in the *New York Times* and by debates on Facebook.

The issue dragged on until in November 2014 Hachette books were delivered just as before. Hachette still determines the selling price of its books and receives an incentive from Amazon when it lowers the price of its books.

The result is that Hachette now bets on multiple channels (online) to sell books and works on increasing knowledge of readers and their preferences. The multi-channel policy will still rely heavily on Amazon but it has now been warned.

Due to this conflict publishers are on guard, and we are only at the beginning of a long road strewn with channel conflicts. The battle will involve who owns which customer knowledge and who determines the retail price of books.

Chapter 3

Costs for making a book

Approximately 50% of the sales price (ie. the transfer price) is for the publisher. But how is this amount put together? The chain of actions that add value to the original, author-created story consists of the following components:

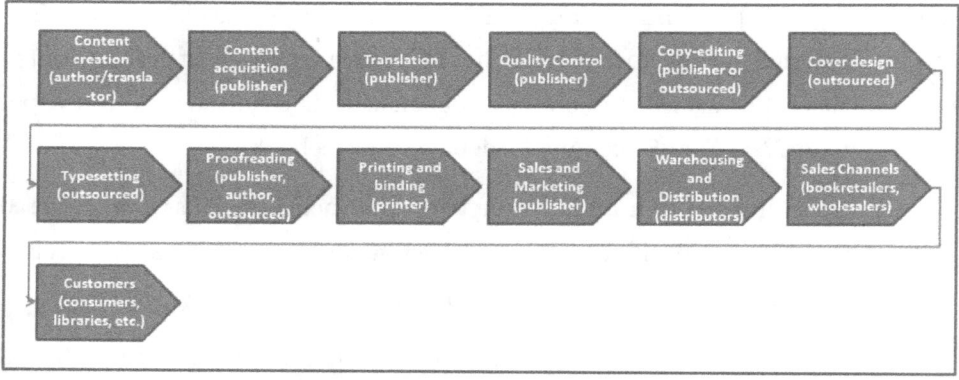

Fig. 3.1 The publishing value chain (from: Thompson, Merchants of Culture)

On the issue of "tinkering with the text" the publishing value chain seems a bit out of balance compared to all other parts. But it also shows that in the linguistic world of the book quality at that point is perceived as very important. Obviously there is a lot to say about the process that is presented here. On all parts of the process there is much to say and of course also much to improve and standardize. We'll talk about it further on in the chapters on the various cost components.

The value chain I have somewhat simplified and incorporated into a picture of the cost structure to be able to follow it better numerically. It looks like this:

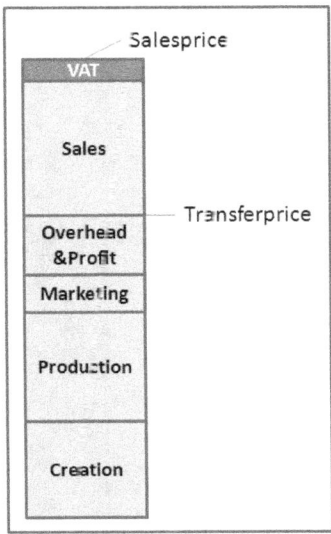

Fig. 3.2 Cost structure of a P-book

The figure is set up for the P-book. The tricky part here is that a lot of the costs are given for both P-books as for E-books, and they are not always easy to separate nor simply to allocate to. The allocation of these costs to a title is always a basis for controversy. For example, many publishers charge the costs such as copy-editing and translation of the text to the P-book. The E-book seems therefore much more profitable because the costs are indeed already attributed elsewhere. A fair cost attribution on both types of production is of course possible but usually can only be done afterwards. Therefore, we limit ourselves here to costs across the P-book. Later we discuss the typical cost elements of the E-book and some considerations about the distribution and attribution of costs over P- and E-books.

Distribution of costs in practice

What emerges from our benchmark in the next chapter is an interesting breakdown of all costs on the products. Please note: this is an average over 14 publishers, large and small:

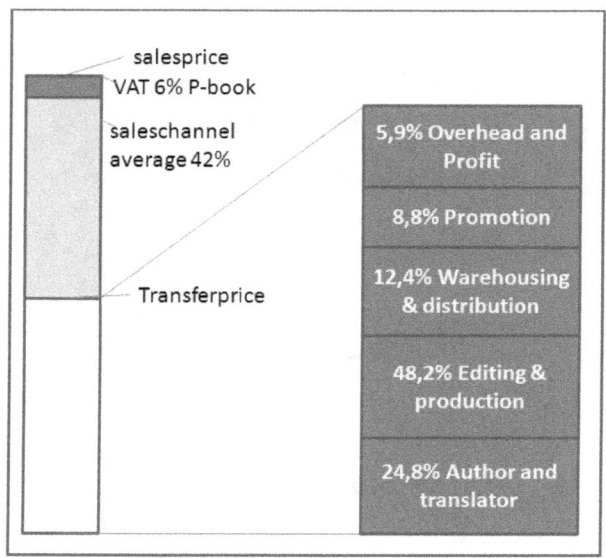

Fig. 3.3 Break down of the transfer price from the benchmark

More than a quarter of the transfer fee goes to the author (royalties and advances) and the translator (in translated works). Nearly half to the efforts to make it a publishable manuscript (part editing, formatting, cover design) and to print. More than 12% goes to warehousing and distribution costs to salesoutlets (in the Netherlands this is often at the Centraal Boekhuis or Central Book Depot), about 9% on average is spent on promotion and marketing, and so there remains 5.9% for not directly attributable costs to the book like costs of the publishing house (buildings, the secretary and the director, IT costs), and the resulting margin or profit.

In essence, this does not say much about the efficiency of the average publishing company in the Netherlands. If we accept the argument that these amounts are the same for all the books in the Netherlands , it is noticeable that there are a lot of costs involved in making the product itself (48.2%), which is pretty much produced for stock and the storage of that stock (which is waste in the pure sense of the word), that promotion is on average not bad but relatively low (but still requires further comparison). A contribution of 6% to cover overhead and profit is far too little. The snapshot in this benchmark indicates that in general publishing in the Netherlands is not profitable.

Profit levels

I don't want to debate whether the fees and profit levels are reasonable or not. Suffice it here to note that publishers take risks in bringing out a book and do capital investments to do so. The return on that capital investment must contain some reasonability.

If enormous profits would be made, one has to deal with inexorable economic laws that say that you are going to have heavy competition so your profits will automatically shrink or that prices will fall and thus the market secures a correction. That is essentially what happened in the last decades of the last century. Competing on price was not really possible due to the law on the fixed book price, but tougher competition was obviously something that was advancing.

The publisher guild has long complained bitterly about the bids that it has to do for manuscripts of authors and that prices are getting higher. Particularly in the Anglo-Saxon part of the market there is a huge upward pressure on purchase of content, ie authors require greater advances and shares of profits, thanks to the rising power of agents in the English language. These ask continually higher prices for foreign rights (also for the Dutch market) and that obviously has an impact on the cost component of the Dutch publishers, and thus on profit levels.

But if those profits are too low you get the reaction that we have seen in recent years and which can be summed up as the race to the bottom: consolidation and mergers of independent publishing houses in large companies on the one hand and on the other hand contraction if that consolidation does not yield enough 'economies of scale'. The pressure of new possibilities such as E-books - the Internet as a disruptive basis for new distribution partners like Amazon - should prepare the publishing community for a new approach to the book. However, in practice, this hasn't happened yet.

Until recently a profitability of around 10% before tax was a reasonable starting point for publishers that publish for the consumermarket. That 10% has only been achieved in recent years in exceptional cases. This explains why the entire industry is in such turmoil. At the time that 10% was still achieved, it was not so much invested in development and renewal of the publishing house itself, for example in improving the production and inventory process or customer knowledge and marketing knowledge and innovative capabilities; but rather it was partially invested in acquisitions and mergers into larger conglomerates (eg, in the Netherlands VBK, WPG, Lannoo) but hardly in innovations in order to sustain growth or to absorb bad times. When that 10% margin began to dwindle in the crisis, it was a major reason why many publishers went down and large conglomerates were having very difficult times.

There is plenty to improve to turn the tide. Obviously, the condition is that released funds are spent on professional development and smart investments in innovative environments that support a clear strategy for the future. More on that later in the chapters on strategy.

That there is confusion about how costs and revenues are allocated for a P-book is shown by an article in the leading Dutch newspaper *NRC* (February 21, 2014) which asked the publishers themselves how the cost structure per book looked like. Whether they knew the right amounts I doubt it, but the resulting image gives a distorted image at least when compared with the benchmark data that provide more details.

In my honest opinion the warehousing part of the costs have been grossly overlooked by the sources of the newspaper; a problem many publishers overlook unfortunately. Also direct overhead contributions, editingcosts and production preparation and sales effort have been typically neglected.

After the article the image remained that the publishers were making huge profits by publishing a book; this book will show that much more nuance is needed and the world is much less rosy, too.

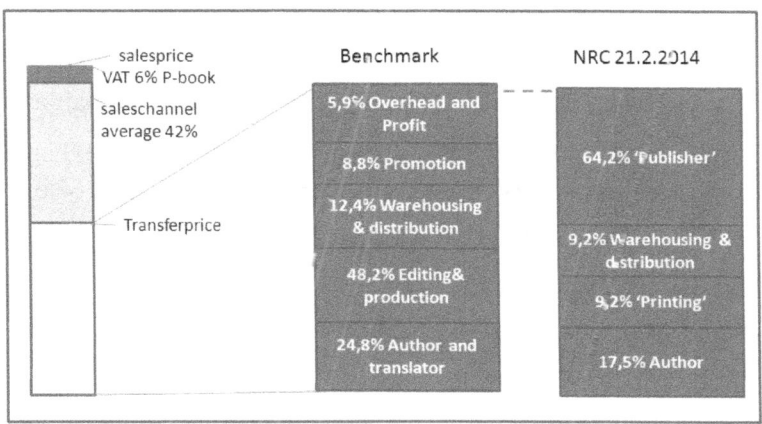

Figuur 3.4 Cost structure compared to the NRC article (21-2-2014)

First let's look at some more details of the costs of each book described above.

Chapter 4

Author costs and translation costs

An author has copyright in the Netherlands on his workt. He usually yields the use or operating rights to his publisher, for which he receives royalties. Royalties are given usually in the form of a percentage of the price of the book minus VAT, paid per copy sold. Sometimes the author will receive an advance before the book was published (or even conceived) to ensure that the publisher has an exclusive right until the book was published. The advance is usually deducted from the revenue (royalties).

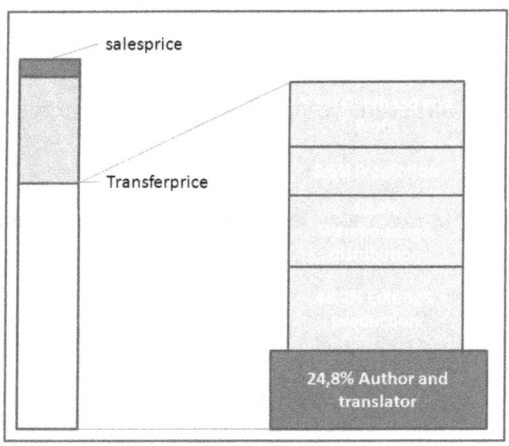

Fig. 4.1 Author and transalation costs

In the Netherlands, the Dutch Publishers Association (NUV) has drawn up a model contract for writers in which everything is settled about the exploitation of rights and ancillary rights (for stage, film, merchandise, and more). Virtually all publishers use it. Particularly bestselling authors negotiate their own contracts, but the bulk of writers in the Netherlands recognizes the model contract.

Risk

The author's publisher receives via the model contract an exclusive right to exploit the book. He thus stands as a risk operator between the distribution channel, manufacturing suppliers, marketers, etc., and the author, and he takes all the hassle away for the author. If the author would not want this arrangement, he himself would have to negotiate, implement and maintain all contracts with suppliers and distribution channels. In this way, the author theoretically could indeed earn more. The emerging self publishing industry is set to achieve this: that the author pays for production, marketing and distribution services to his own needs. The risk is therefore for himself. In the chapters on strategy I'll elaborate further on that.

Royalty percentages

Back to the current practice: it is striking the NUV assumes that per publishing format (paperback, hardcover, paperback or mid-price) separate royalty percentages apply. That has to do with the assumption that the sales prices and margins vary by publishing format (and thus by the stage of the life cycle of a title) in such a way that there must be a reasonable distribution of revenues between publisher and author. The average percentages used in the Netherlands are in the figure below, noting that in practice lower percentages are common especially for pockets (5 to 6% rather than 8 to 10%).

In my model for the benchmark later in the book we use the NUV percentages. In practice this does not apply to bestselling writers obviously , because they often get higher amounts, especially higher advances.

The benchmark model therefore gives a slightly distorted image, which can be remedied by recognizing that heavily profitable bestseller titles in terms of earnings are again skimmed by the author, whether or not aided by his agent.

Paperback or Hard Cover	Mid-price	Pocket
1 - 4000_____10% 4001 - 10.000_____12,5% 10.001 - 100.000___15% above 100.000____17,5%	1 - 3000_____9% 3001 - 50.000_____10% above 50.000____12,5%	1 - 30.000_____8% above 30.000_____10%

Fig. 4.2 Royalty rates per copy sold on the basis of the selling price, source:
NUV, 2014

Striking features

What's even more striking is that the publisher is deemed to be paid out over the (fixed) end user price of each copy, minus VAT and not the transfer price of the book to the sales channel. Compared to many other countries this is exceptional.

The entrepreneur, ie. the publisher is considered to pay out to the author a significant proportion of the selling price in the shop (approximately 40%, as we noted) over which he has no formal influence. A situation has risen in which the manufacturer (the publisher) pays the author money on sales that he has not received.

Whether the publisher reasons in the same manner towards the sales channel is doubtful. From the past, there seems to be a somewhat protective attitude towards the sales channel (ie the bookstore).

The right to return, the fixed book price, the assumption of risk towards authors: these are all elements that hinder the prospect of a more or less normal market functioning and entrepreneurial responsibility for both the publisher and the distributor.

This has created a situation between bookstores and publishers where publishers in the course of time have assumed a lot of responsibility without direct control, while the bookstore gained a lot of power over publishers: the bookstore picks and chooses titles from the systematic oversupply (overproduction) in titles from the publishers.

By lack of alternative distribution channels and the dominance of the bookstores as a channel an interdependence developed between publishers and booksellers. The bankruptcy and failed restart of Polare (a large bookchain in the Netherlands) in 2014 and the arm twisting that the owners of the chain excercised over the publishers (they argued that the publishers had to pay a share of the resulting deficit) invoked the refusal of those same publishers to help in the failure of Polare, may be seen as a break in the trend of interdepence.

Case: Authors earn below the minimum wage

In the summer of 2014, a report was published by the British Authors' Licensing & Collection Society (ALCS), similar to the Vereniging van Letterkundigen (VvL, Dutch Society of Literary Scholars) in the Netherlands. The British investigated among 2454 authors many issues a.o. income.

It turned out that in eight years the income of these authors (including inflation) had dropped with almost 30% from £ 12,330 in 2005 to £ 11,000 in 2014. The minimum income of a single-person household in England is £ 16,850 pounds.

The proportion of the population who considers writing his or her sole profession had dropped to 11.5 percent, where it was still 40% in 2005. Most writers earned their money by writing for publications on paper; there were almost no authors that had an income with digital publications.

The ALCS had also asked authors whether self publishing was an alternative. Of the interviewed 25% admitted to have published a book themselves costing them an average of 500 pounds. The financial revenues were approximately 700 pounds, making the return on investment a sheer 40%. The vast majority of these self-publishers (89%) considered to proceed with this type of publishing.

The study also looked at the contracts of self-published authors. Of those surveyed more than 69% said that they could preserve the copyrights. 'Retaining copyrights gives authors a much stronger negotiating position in the area of how their work can be used', says the study. 'The best contracts set out clearly the rights that the authors retain or transfer.'

The Netherlands

The latest figures from the Dutch VvL are from 2005/2006, when the average income of authors was still at € 18,000 to € 19,000. The 1612 authors surveyed worked an average 19 hours per week.

Whether the comparison with England holds is hard to say, because in the Netherlands a safety net exists in the form of the Nederlands Letterenfonds (Dutch Foundation for Literature), which provides grants and scholarships to writers. This does obviously not apply to all writers who earn on average € 18 gross per hour with their occupation as a quick calculation based on the above shows. On top of that the income of the average author drops, shown by the fact that sales of books as a whole fell by 25% in the last five years. If you would apply that to author income the aforementioned € 18 is but a little over € 14, not counting inflation.

Translation

As shown by figures on the Dutch market, about 70% of the titles for the consumer market is translated from a foreign language. It entails significant costs. For these costs again the NUV publishes (to be precise the Literary publishing group within the NUV, together with the Association of Writers and Translators) the so called "reasonable rates for the translation of literary works." In 2014 it stood at 6.4 eurocents per translated word. These are recommended rates, so it allows publishers and translators to waive them. For a work of 50,000 words, it boils down to a cost for the publisher of € 3,200.

Given the often very time-consuming work for the translator also this part of the publishing industry is not exactly paradise. Again incentives exist in the form of grants from the Dutch Foundation for Literature but as with every title not every translator can rely on that. In a very enlightening report from 2011, compiled by the Flemish Authors' Association, an insight is given into how the translator guild is doing. On average, a translator spends 21 hours a week on his work; it is not surprising that translators virtually all have a different job on top of it; 79% of the participants in the Flemish report indicates that he/she cannot make ends meet by translating only.

Chapter 5

Editing

In this book 'editorial effort' is defined to be all the costs that have to do with selecting and creating the book and the coordination of the editing process by the publisher.

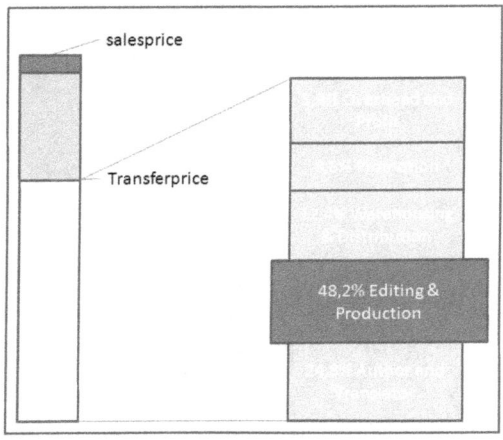

Fig. 5.1 Editorial and production costs

The editorial effort consists of guiding authors to improve their script and to edit the text in such a way that it is publishable. The pre-selection of authors is a major, time-consuming activity for the publisher. But a very important one. There are basically three ways for a publisher to get a script:

.by receiving unsolicited manuscripts

.to invite writers to deliver a book

.by acquisition, whether or not through agents

Slushpile

The Netherlands has an estimated one million or more people trying to write a book. Some send his or her unsolicited manuscript to a publisher hoping it will be published. Hundreds of manuscripts end up with publishers every year. If not directly thrown into the dustbin, the remainder ends up in principle in a big pile, which is called the slushpile. Only very few manuscripts are ultimately wholly viewed and judged. It is an almost impossible task to check each and every story.

I once met an editor who read some 200 manuscripts in its entirety every year. That was even without all the texts he stopped reading after one or two pages. He read those manuscripts outside working hours because he did not have enough time during the day! Some publishers are also using external editors and freelancers who make reports of such manuscripts. These are external costs that often end up in the overhead allocation of the publisher. In short, the chance to be published by the unsolicited presentation of a manuscript is very small.

Sometimes a publisher or editor asks an author to write a book, perhaps because he thinks a subject is interesting enough and considers the author to be a good match for it. This for example is often used for non-fiction or books where current affairs and actuality play an important role. But it could also be that a publisher wants to encourage an author by challenging him to write a book.

In addition, many manuscripts are purchased. This can be through the intercession of third parties, such as agents or consultants with other (mostly foreign) publishers, or through any agent representing writers and who basically function as selectors for publishers. The role of agents seems to be smaller for the Dutch language market than in countries such as the UK and the USA.

Quality

Most authors feel that their manuscript - once it's finalised - is immediately ready for printing. But a publisher or the editor often have written and unwritten rules about the quality they pursue. First, it can be about the technical editing of a text, meaning the spelling, punctuation and the like.

But it can also refer to the content of the story, the development of the characters, the crucial moments in the narrative description. It can also be about the overall writing style. An editor will always do his best to provide an author with constructive criticism in order to arrive at a quality that the editor or the publisher approves of. Sometimes many revisions are needed to reach a final text.

On closer examination, these revisions are costly in time and handling. There's a lot of time used in the 'traffic' component, say the 'hunting for texts' and telephone communication between editor and author. The turnaround time is also clouded by a manuscript often adjusted during a review round. That does not have to be a problem were it not that the editor sometimes has already ordered the typesetter to start his work and costs are made. Every change in the text afterwards means a change in the work done by others and extra costs are incurred.

Then there is the maintenance of the network of authors and agents, an important task for publishers and editors. The hackneyed joke that publishing is mainly going to lunch with authors is a far cry from reality. It is hard work and the agendas are crowded. Guiding both Dutch and foreign authors is time consuming. Whether it is done in an efficient way, is another question.

Cost allocation

Every effort as part of the foregoing should be considered as part of the cost of the product, but in practice that is often not the case. By author and by manuscript the effort in time may differ seriously. A form of "activity-based costing' would be useful to visualize directly attributable costs. Time recording is no common practice in this industry, let alone standardization of the process at this level (for example: "There is maximum x-amount of time available per page to editors and support for an author who has never published before").

Standardization and time recording would considerably help the transparency of costs. Now for example all efforts of staff and preselection costs are taken in overhead costs and not in the direct costs of the product. The possibility of waste locked in this unattributable cost part is difficult to visualize but in general it is added very handsomely on the 'overheadpile', thereby tarnishing the profit margin.

In the editing process more attention should be given to some regulation and standardization of cost components for the acquisition and improvement and editing of the products. It can be done in various ways such as by differentiating efforts depending on the perceived attractiveness of the work. Or a publisher could for example, choose to spend more time on new authors, if that model would help in training and educating authors.

Because every publisher has different work processes for our benchmark we only included an editorial cost that does not take into account multiple revisions and traffic efforts. The latter means communicating with authors and the tracking and management of other parts of the production effort. A large part of the efforts and costs of the editor is technically included in the overhead costs.

Case: the editor and his work

Regarding the role of the editor and what the profession entails, Jasper Henderson describes in an article in the *Groene Amsterdammer* *. The article refers to the book by Lisa Kuitert 'About editors', in which the profession of editor is regarded as a relatively recent activity.

Early 20th century editor work still consisted of some small editorial services for the respective author as a kind of private editor. Henderson says: "Big publishers in the Netherlands like De Bezige Bij, Querido and Van Oorschot had no editors employed at all, errors were equally removed in the typesetting room and that was pretty much it.

Kuitert writes: "From the late sixties onwards editors enter the field, such as Gerrit Komrij and Martin Ros at Arbeiderspers, Tilly Hermans and Walter Donath Tieges at Meulenhoff and Oscar Timmers and Alice Toledo at de Bezige Bij. It was a new kind of function, whose contours were not quite fixed. "[...]"

The time of an editor according to Henderson is spent on "meetings, writing promotional texts and other office things." But the most important part of the work is for most editors still editing, that is to improve a book.

The role of the editor has changed over the last years. The author puts more and more different demands on the editor. The center of gravity has shifted to being a point of contact for all matters governed by a publishing house, such as: advertising, marketing, sales. "The editor is considered to have an opinion and knowledge about all these matters, to make proposals, in short: to feed everything and everyone constantly."

From " A hopeless dilemma. The (alleged) demise of the editor " by Jasper Henderson, De Groene Amsterdammer, August 11, 2010.

Chapter 6

Production Effort

If the publisher has decided to invest in the product and to produce it, the text is formatted to a type page and type set so that it can be printed. The sort of paper is determined, the cover is designed and the whole is printed. For electronic versions all formatting issues are of less importance and there are no costs for paper and printing. Adjusting the text to E-book format can be a wholly automated operation.

All these processes are typically not in place at the publishing house itself but outsourced. Costs are usually dependent on what the publisher has been able to negotiate with suppliers. In benchmarks, which are often used to make sure that costs are not too high and show market conformity, it appears that especially small and medium-sized publishing houses sometimes pay too much. The large conglomerates are often in a better position to negotiate better contracts. Typesetters and printers in the Netherlands (and indeed worldwide) have considerable excess capacity; hence there is always something to negotiate on prices.

Cover

Considerable time is spent on the design of the cover. That is not surprising when considering that many readers base their purchasing decisions for P-books on the cover. Research shows that in a mere 25% of cases, the cover determines the purchase (the biggest reason for purchases by the way are recommendations from people they know, in over 30% of cases).

Cover panel tests are sometimes held to assess acceptance by the public. There is a lot involved when it comes to the attraction of the book to the prospective buyer. Use of color and visual language may be crucial for recognition on the shelves of bookstores. Because often from the outside the quality of the story or the content of the story cannot be discerned, the psychology of the image and the impression of the cover is one of the few factors you can use as a publisher. Whether all effort spent is really of help remains to be seen.

Also for E-books, the cover can be an important item. In their book, *Author, Publisher, Entrepreneur* Guy Kawasaki and Shawn Welch leave no ambiguity about how important the cover of a book is if one has to look at a (small) screen to choose between different small thumbnails, representing book covers. Their tip: use a large font for the title so that even in a greatly reduced thumbnail the title can still be read. Or even create different covers for P-book and E-book.

Paper

Cost of paper itself is often low. Especially if the book does not involve a richly illustrated edition. Again, standardization at this level will help to keep costs manageable. The time that a publisher meddles with the "opacity" (transparency) of paper is over in my honest opinion.

Also on standardization of the interior (the type page layout and font) and form standardization (the format of the printed book) one can reach consensus eventually - albeit reluctantly and with a huge amount of resistance from the more traditional faction within the publishing house and with authors.

The savings from type page layout and shape standardization require little explanation. After all, texts will be typeset automatically, which can save a lot of money and by form standardization one can realise clear contracts with printers and finishers.

Print run

The main discussion will almost always end up on the determination of the (paper) edition: the amount of copies to be printed in a book. (E-books logically speaking don't have this problem).

At this point it is important to note that the printing of an edition usually makes heavy demands on the capital of a publishing house. By clever negotiating a publisher can indeed bring down the cost per paper book, but as the printing of a book, for example, costs € 1.50 per copy, and one prints 5,000, the company invests a sum of € 7,500 and with 50,000 copies over €75,000.

Cost prices are lower by larger issues and it is often dependent on what process is used (printing, offset printing, print on demand (POD)) and the finish (sewn, stitched, glued, etc.) is selected. It is often a matter of cents per copy, but with a print run of 5000 or 15 000 it affects the total capital requirement.

Precalculation, postcalculation

In principle, the assignment process in most publishing houses are along the lines of what we call P & L: Profit & Loss forms looking like small businessplans per book. Precalculations, they are also called. When correct it not only contains the needed circulation, but also the marketing efforts, promotion costs and the like.

The problem is that many publishers do not see the P & L as a tool to get a better grip on the business. There are even publishers who artificially overestimate the print runs in that they can artificially decrease the cost price per book. Therewith creating a larger use of capital than needed, because the print run is larger then they realistically can sell. Postcalculations (a kind of retrospective analysis of the differences with the precalculation) are often skipped and that is very unfortunate. The instrument of estimating and costing is a normal entrepreneurial way of risk assessment. Doing a postcalculation should lead to an understanding of the profitability of the decisions of a publisher and might even be able to form an assessment method or tool for compensation for that same publisher.

Most precalculations are therefore estimates, and represent as I said a significant business risk. The way this risk is handled hampers the way in which publishing is currently practiced. It can really only be reduced by better decisions to support shorter print runs, by standardizing production and by adopting tiered pricing. Or by deciding not to publish the book at all.

Circulation determination

How many books do you sell in the end? That is the key question in determining the print run. First, we noted earlier that there is no real understanding of the customers buying behaviour. The comprehensive,' fact-based ' marketing in other markets, such as the Fast Moving Consumer Goods, is generally lacking in the book publishing environment. Large publishers in the Netherlands have an odd business analyst employed, but smaller publishers have no active demand for this type of activity. The lack of this insight results in 'producing for stock' and that 'feeling' and 'experience' are playing important roles. These last two elements have suffered badly the past years because sales haven't reached the numbers that they had some years ago. Also promotion in television programs such as *De Wereld Draait Door (DWDD)*, (translated: the world keeps turning), a very popular TV show with the exact target audience for books and for its high viewing figures often an important promotional body, is no guarantee for success and numbers. An author who had been in *DWDD* told me that despite his TV appearance in the program no more than 500 books of his work sold, where there were 5000 envisaged.

Publishers who year after year released successful books but suddenly hardly have any noteworthy title in the market: it is common, and the unspoken fear of the publisher lies in "losing the instinct." You could say that it looks like the publishing decision itself needs some rationalisation. Nobody dares to say so, but being simply lucky in the current approach to publishing and marketing might be greater than one would like. The luck factor is a subject I'll return to later on.

Waste

The disadvantage of in-stock production is that there are also costs to be incurred in the rest of the process: in particular, the cost of storage of books not (yet) sold can be devastating, as discussed below. Waste is lurking.

Conversely, it is also a problem that if a book sells well a printer can not always reprint immediately: the principle of batchproduction, what a printing company does, creates a certain lead time, changeover time and waiting time before the machines can produce the book again. It can take days, but also weeks, depending on the contract, the pricing and possibilities with the printer.

Another thorny issue in the process of making a book is the power or rather the lack thereof, of those who are responsible for coordinating the production process within the publishing company. Traditionally, the responsible for production is on the lowest rung of the ladder in the publishing house. He is not seen in contrast to more IT-oriented publishing environments such as education or STM as a serious partner in efficiency matters.

Case: How important is good circulation policy

A harrowing but familiar example of how important a good circulation policy is is illustrated in the graph below. The sales of a book showing a typical cycle in which the publisher is often asked to print extra at a certain time or not. In the graph it is clear that the initial estimates have been extremely good but when it comes to printing a next batch the conservative calculation is totally and completely out of sight. The costs this entails is one of the biggest money wasters.

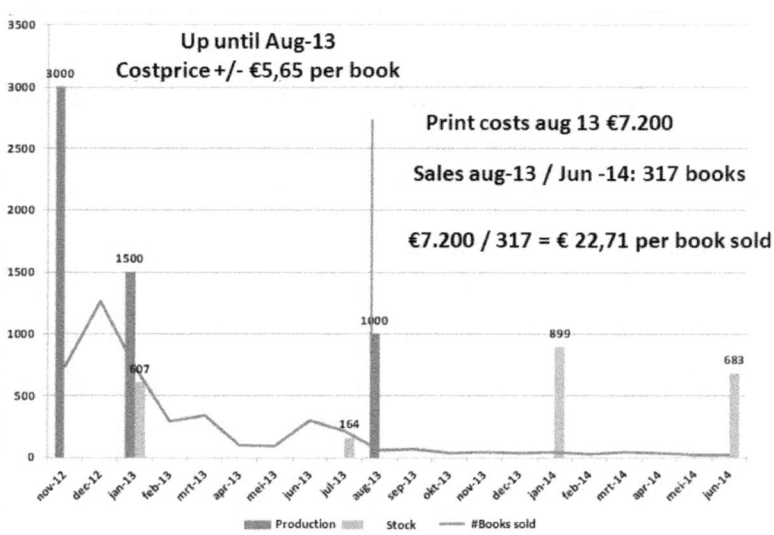

Fig. 6.1 Circulation Determination

As you can see there is far too much reprinted at the time the title has reached the end of its lifecycle. The amounts here are fictitious, but it is clear that by inaccurate estimates the once profitable product can suddenly become a lossmaker. And we're not talking about storage costs here, which will even press harder on this title if the stock is not shredded fast.

Production lessons

The lessons you can draw from this is that conservative purchasing is important; do not produce based on wishful thinking. Additionally, to change modes of production is a key tactic, with maxims:

.offset printing when you are sure and when you need quantities

.printing with low predictability

.printing on demand (POD) when a product is no longer available and there is little sign of increased sales But also for a first run when unsure about the success of the title or author.

56

Other ways of delivery

Other ways of agreements with the printers and distribution channels should stimulate more demand-driven manufacturing. A 'just-in-time' (JIT) way of producing and delivering the product would have to prevent stockpiling. That seems absurd, but it is not: the lessons of the automotive industry, where complex products are also made on a daily basis, should help here. And supermarket chains have adopted JIT already as a standard. There's a small consolation: these two industries have invested in this process for several years before the JIT process went smoothly.

Apart from piles of books that one needs up-front in the store as push-material, it is a small effort in today's Internet age to followup an order in the shop with fine mazed distribution, if necessary on the doorstep of the customer.The whole phenomenon of online ordering entails that the production line can be linked to it. Based on the ordering behavior with the producer one can decide whether to deliver the order using POD or you by producing on stock and deliver from there. The savings on printing and storage costs are enormous. The benefits for the marketers of both the bookstore and the publisher (you get a name and address plus ordering behavior) are also significant. The Dutch return rule, where distributors can return excess books to the publisher without any cost would thus have a more mature character. The risk in the current situation is pressing too heavily on the publisher.

Chapter 7

Warehousing and distribution

The costs for storage and distribution of books (transport to retail, mostly shops and bookstores) in the Netherlands are for the most part determined by the Central Book House (Centraal Boekhuis - CB), a unique joint institution of bookstores and publishers. Most publishers use the CB as their warehouse. The rates of the CB can be found on the internet but they are not easy to grasp; they are amongst others strongly determined by the turnover rate, the size of the publisher (relatively lower costs for larger publishers), and the volume occupied by a book. The printers deliver their books in bulk at the warehouse of the CB and the CB delivers it in smaller quantities at the bookstore. Any returns are again handled by CB.

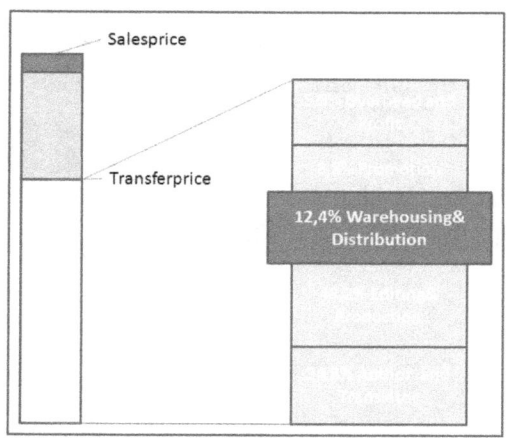

Fig7.1 Warehousing and distribution costs

Inventory costs

Inventory costs can really add up with the number of titles it contains and the amount of unsold books, produced on stock. The CB has made a considerable investment in a print-on-demand facility and is capable of handling titles as single copies, if needed directly to the consumer. In addition, the CB also provides E-books online to customers such as bookstores but also to individual customers.

The tricky thing with inventory costs is that it really is dead capital that can not be used for other things. This locked-in capital is waste in its purest form. This waste is very low if a book sells well. Instead, it is a 'double whammy' if the book is not selling well and if there is a considerable stock of the title. Next to the print run the publisher needs to finance and should depreciate, there are also still relatively high inventory costs. Sometimes it can not be done otherwise, for example, more expensive books with lots of color and illustrations that have to be printed. In that case printing for stock is ususally the cheapest way. The active clearing and managing of inventory is a significant and often underestimated task.

Distribution costs

As described above distribution costs of the P-book mainly contain the costs incurred from the CB to the middlemen. But due to increased online delivery and the previously mentioned just in time production methods another delivery component will be added when it comes to the type of direct distribution to the consumer. It brings a fine-meshed logistical operation to the consumer or to the pickup point for those same consumers.

Significant savings in stock and circulation will have to outweigh the distribution costs and the POD cost. It is clear that the distribution channel that masters this game best can benefit considerably. Namely the distribution channel can learn a lot about the consumers and their preferences and benefit from them. Whether the logistical operation will remain a role for the CB or that that role will be taken over by inventive printers remains to be seen.

Case: Example of changes in distribution

In the spring of 2014 the publisher de Bezige Bij delivered - in exchange for more and better shelf space plus a 3% higher margin in some bookstores - directly to a selected number of bookstores outside the CB. Particularly well selling titles and a number of smaller titles that strengthened the Bezige Bij portfolio. De Bezige Bij was pretty open in its communication, where other publishers - albeit on a very small scale - already did this. According to the arrangement between CB, bookstore and publisher a publisher can deliver outside the CB to customers directly, but does it make sense? Let's make a small calculation:

3% more margin for the bookstore costs the publisher 60 cents extra per book at a book sale price of € 20. Distribution expenses from the printer to the bookstores will eventually boil down to a few cents per book, so a few ten euro's per pallet. But the same amount of distribution costs had to be paid by de Bezige Bij to the CB if they had done it the old way (plus the cost of transport from the printer to the CB). A pallet of -in this example - 200 books cost a maximum total of € 200. Of this amount, € 120 goes to the bookstore (200 times 60 cents) and the publisher has bought an extra amount of attention and shelf space in the store. Both bookstore and publisher now run the risk that the supply of the CB will be more expensive because smaller titles will be distributed in smaller batches, which are more expensive because these titles are not co-packaged with well selling titles. It is interesting to see if the printer can replace the required distribution tasks of the CB, and whether the printer can as efficiently distribute at competitive costs. After all, usually this printer only had one adress to send his goods to, being it the CB. Now he must offer the same distribution granularity as the CB to the bookstore.

In short, in the US a publisher pays about $ 1 per book for a premium spot in the store (see, among others, Thompson, Merchants of Culture). This is apparently also becoming the norm in the Netherlands. Whether it is smart to sacrifice a long-term cooperation (with other bookstores and publishers in the CB) for that amount for short-term gain remains to be seen.

Chapter 8

Promotion

In publishing promotion is also called marketing or PR. Actually it is marketing promotion or publicity, and certainly not marketing as practiced by other industries. Publicity is certainly well established with publishers when it comes to traditional channels such as advertising and free publicity. The social media are used more and more, but it is typically used to 'send' the publishers'message and the search is still going on to establish more of a 'dialogue' with customers.

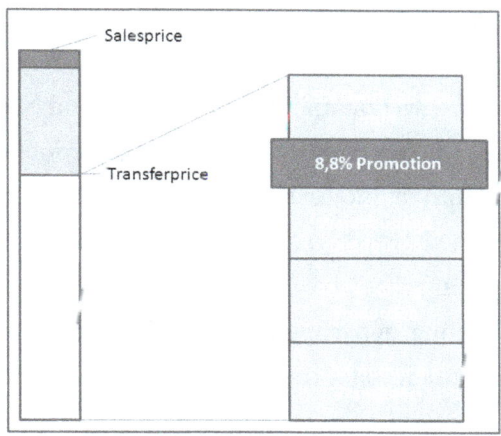

Fig. 8.1 Promotion costs

That also has to do with a generation of publishers and writers who did not grow up with social media as a tool for self-promotion. Groups of writers decline this form of publicity, thinking the role of the publisher is to "push"their product. At the same time there is a group of writers that use social media actually better than their publishers and have more feeling with 'self promotion'.

But marketing in the sense of understanding what customers want, developing products likewise and tuning the whole marketingmix seems still far away. Traditional product push by constantly drawing the attention of the customer towards a product, will still persist for a long time. Especially with bestsellers from well known authors, but for smaller titles and lesser known writers it is no longer sufficient.

Knowledge about customers

Promoting a book is always hard work, and even harder in the current age of fragmented media attention. The lack of knowledge and lack of data at the micro-level of target readers is felt in these markets, with writers and themes that make them difficult to sell.

Real hard data about purchasing and reading habits only major online distributors such as Amazon and Bol.com have. They are not very willing to share that information (yet?) with publishers. Having sociodemographic (hard data on end-users) and socio-psychographic (behavioral and preference data) of audiences is a battle that the publishers have long overlooked. In the time that money flowed abundantly marketing databases were deemed not necessary: the supply market functioned properly. Now that the supply market has increasingly turned into a demand market and has at the same time also shrunk, having a state of the art marketing department is actually indispensable. And I do not mean marketing promotion, but strategic marketing and marketing or business intelligence, the function to turn customer data into useful recommendations about which products to make and how to raise awareness.

Publishers do not like to invest in this kind of activity. Many publishers seem to want to maintain the illusion that the market for books and reading is different from all other markets. But one will have to go with the flow, because the risk of issuing bad selling titles is disproportionately big if the publisher has no idea who the customers are, how many there are and what they want. To rely on serendipity, chance of success, that we wrote about in the chapter on circulation provision, can become very costly. Good marketing has a restraining effect on that uncertainty.

Promotion budgets

The average of 9% for promotion to which the benchmark concludes is difficult to assess as long as the context is missing: differentiation by marketing (communication) effort for each target group and each book is of paramount importance.

Elberse argues that making a blockbuster is a matter of spending considerable marketing and promotional budgets; she believes in 'forcing' a success. In the Netherlands we have enough examples, for example in the entertainment world. All the musicals of Joop van de Ende have huge up-front investments of which marketing budgets are written in double digit percentage-figures of turnover throughout the life cycle of a production. The flops of TV programs at the same time show that success is not always enforced by money. but that you can steer success to a certain extent with a substantial promotional budget.

Sensible marketing

The parallel is quickly made to books and therewith to the 'bestseller' market. In the bookmarket great marketing efforts aren't focused on only a few titles but budgets are fragmented over (too) many titles. And even with big titles the same script is used over and over again; a presentation here, a full-page advertisement there, some book presentations and interviews and - to keep it cheap - as much free publicity as possible. If Joop van den Ende was a publisher he'd do it otherwise.

Sensible targetgroup development and database building seems the motto for the next few years for publishers, with a clear vision on profiles online. Even adopting a social media strategy blindly is not a panacea for all ills: a good online strategy is also based on target group knowledge and insight. For example, if the target is above 65 for a particular title you should ask yourself seriously whether that effort pays off or if it's better if a different media mix is chosen.

To achieve such a targetgroup approach is a clear focus on specific genres and / or themes is needed. Through research or the use of 'persona' choices can be made for groups and an associated communication mix. Widely used in the Netherlands are the NOM-classification and Motivaction approach. There is also an Australian study with classifications made of end-user interest in genres and themes. In the section on Strategy we'll come back to this.

Chapter 9

Contribution to overhead and profit

There is no rule that says how much profit can be made in publishing a book, but for the average publisher a 10% pre-tax profit is real. That 10% is needed to build capital buffers for the company but also to invest in growth: organic growth by launching new products, markets, automation, internet solutions, etc., or even by acquisitions of other parties, to be able to keep growing.

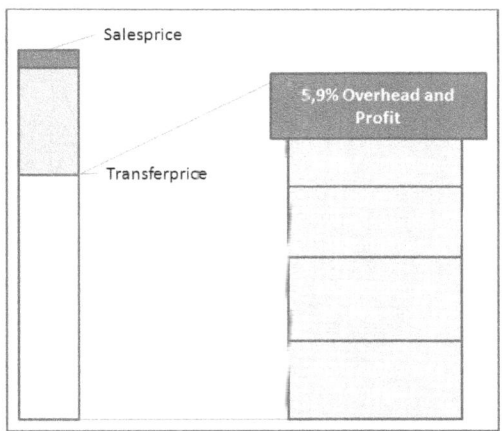

Fig. 9.1 Overhead and Profit

But also the overhead is to be funded and therefore - depending on how a publishing company is organized -extra revenue is needed: for example, the rent of the building and cost of indirect staff (eg a part of staff that is not directly involved like some editors, secretaries, etc.), costs for management and other costs that cannot not directly be allocated on products (books).

In other media industries, such as publishing for professionals and scientists, a contribution to overhead and profit of 15 to 20% is usually the case. It is my observation that the 10% profit contribution in publishing books has hardly happened the past five years - let alone combined with the overhead contribution. It is my perception that restructuring in overhead hasn't been done as strict as possible (and not always in the right places either), making the aforementioned 15-20% impossible. The paltry 6% which emerges from the benchmark speaks volumes. That probably also explains why in recent years the market shrunk and did not grow. There is simply little investment in new opportunities, markets, distribution activities or innovations, because (hopefully) there was a vision but money failed. As innovations often require a long time span, usually a period of three to five years before an innovation really works, you could argue that the publishing industry as a whole has accumulated a backlog of five to 10 years.

It is therefore not surprising that the publisher is vulnerable to new entrants who have no problems, as the wealthy (Amazon, Bol.com and other distribution channels) or starters are trying to be disruptive (Scribd, oyster).

Chapter 10

E-book and cost allocations

In chapter two I already made clear that there are multiple embodiments of the 'narrative experience'. This book is about the P-book and E-book experience. On revenues and expenses I already indicated where relevant elements lie for the P-book cost. For completeness. it is good to dwell on the same elements for the E-book.

In chapter two, I described that the price for an E-book has a different perception to its customers than a P-book, and that price differentiation is big in foreign markets where the E-book has already large salesvclumes.

In the benchmark there are relatively few significant figures for the cost of E-books, in part because the number of E-books in the measured period is not large. The price points are still relatively high. For a P-book of € 20 the price for the E-book version amounts to anywhere between € 11 and € 15.

Other forms of distribution

What I do want to mention is that lending of E-books and 'streaming' offers of large quantities of E-books will influence the market. Since 2014 Amazon offers subscriptions at $ 9.99 per month, for which you can download up to 10 books on a device. To read more titles you have to backload a book and you can again choose a new title.

Because similar lending practices (e.g. in the former lending of DVDs in the music market) ultimately always lead to streaming solutions, one can wait for this type of initiative.

The principle of streaming will invite to publish faster, cheaper, to achieve more knowledge about reading habits and to make more transparent pricing.But no matter what solution or technology will arise: the story will always prevail and must be of good quality; otherwise it will simply not be read.

Cost of an E-book

The cost column for the E-book is as follows (see Figure 10.1), where the percentages are assumptions based on experience in the market. Because the market is moving, the cost prices are also not very stable.

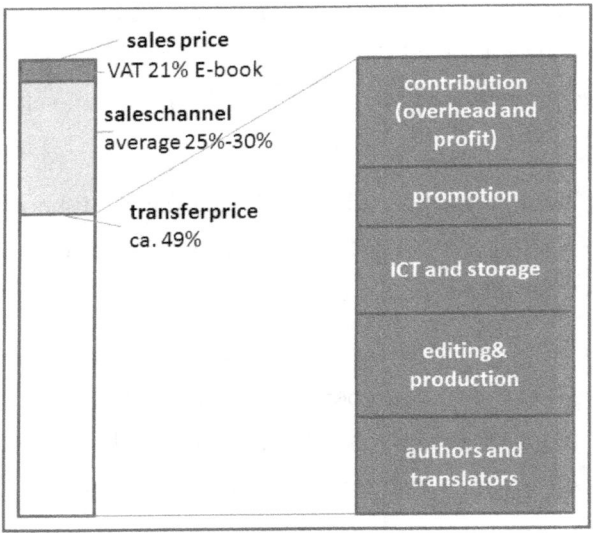

Fig. 10.1 Cost distribution E-book

The transfer price is - relatively, not absolutely! - about the same as a P-book; around 50% of the selling price. This is partly because the higher VAT contribution of 21% is somewhat offset by lower sales channel remittance. The sales channel (usually an online store such as Apple, Bol.com or Amazon) requires between 25% and 30%, which is partly due to the inherent lower cost of electronic distribution of an E-book, but in my honest opinion extremely high for an online distribution cost.

Assuming the same effort for promotion as a P-book, there is less need for distribution and also for parts of the production and multiplication of the E-book. Because everything is done digitally there is almost a negligible cost. To set up an E-book in EPUB format encodings must be done from the text, but because this can usually be done automatically, costs are very low compared with P-books. Usually it is a set-upfee of a few euro's and a fee per word, but there is so much excess capacity that these prices (especially in off shoring) are continuously dropping.

The distribution can take place in many ways, with large differences in pricing. With the CB storage and distribution costs approximate € 1 per title, with other parties (worldwide) pricing is sometimes based on a percentage of sales. All models are available and one can pick and choose, really. The market is still quite fluid.

The effort and associated costs of the collection of user and usage data for marketing purposes can be large. It is an important building block for the development of the digital reading experience. Cost allocations of author efforts in the form of royalties are also fixed in the standards of the NUV and amounts here to around 25% of the transfer price, so in order of what is customary in a P-book. The contribution to overhead and profit in this assumption is almost 30% of the transfer price. That seems to be a significant improvement for the publisher and it is undoubtedly a source for another heated debate on the added value of a publisher.

But there is a serious warning in place: the price level of an E-book is necessarily smaller, the absolute cash contribution is smaller. The investment in additional marketing of an E-book are probably much higher than the 9% average that now exists for P-books and I estimate them on a mere 20% of the transfer price. This is because of the intensive support of an online E-book (if you want to do it well) and said structure of databases and investments in customer tracking systems and customer information. This all comes at the expense of overhead and profit. At least, if E-books are also seen as an opportunity for data collection and used as such by publishers and authors.

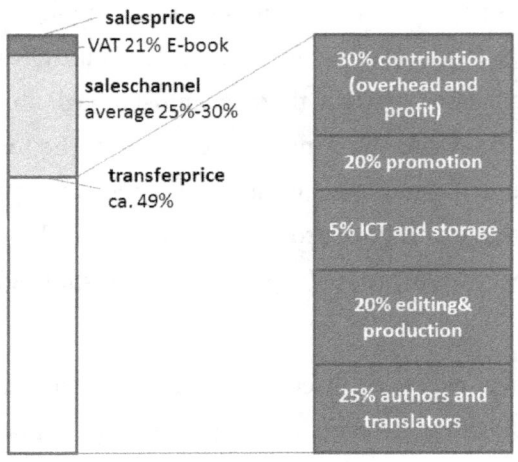

Fig. 10.2 Building blocks E-book costs

Cost breakdown

Gradually we see where the contribution to the editing, translation and production of the story into a book boils down to. In practice, often all costs are allocated to the P-book when it comes to translation and editing costs and often also the promotional costs. For example, an E-book may seem cheap from an accounting point of view, but in practice, the selling price is kept quite high by publishers, therewith making E-books apparently extremely profitable.

The direct production costs for making a book in digital (EPUB) format is an extremely inexpensive operation and that also applies to the storage and distribution costs, as storage and distribution are taking place on the web. It creates the illusion that the publisher swallows a total of more than 65% of the transfer price only to cover some marketing and editorial / translation costs. (NRC February 21, 2014). Many a publisher has seen this pitfall, like publishers for trade and science. They started almost two decades ago with the realization of digital (database) products and at that time they made the classical mistake by allocating all costs on the paper versions of their print products (books, magazines and so-called loose-leaf publications). As a result the electronic versions were thereby highly profitable because prices were kept high.

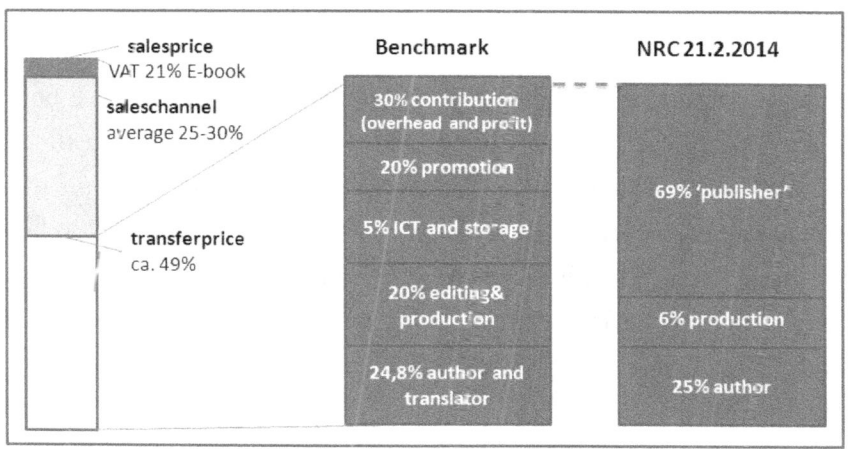

Fig. 10.3 Comparison E-book cost breakdown benchmark and NRC

All creation costs (authors, editors and translations) were not fully allocated to the E-product. Price reductions and sometimes giving away electronic products were then equally in vogue. But it soon appeared that database products were easy to use simultaneously by multiple users. Customers were not obliged any more to buy more than one version of an E-book as was the case with P-books. Publishers quickly stopped that model, and developed licensing models. All this led to achieve a fair valuation and costing of a digital product. Excessive profits were no longer tolerated.

Alternative: selfpublishing

As long as the number of E-books sold is not significantly growing, the publisher will continue to ask his estimated 30% piece of the pie to cover overhead and margin. That's one reason why self-publishing with E-books can be interesting for authors and service providers: the low start-up costs, in particular production and distribution costs can be pocketed by the author or can be 'returned' to the reader in the form of a lower, more realistic price.

Price alternatives

In practice, you see very different price points emerge in which E-books are sometimes offered for: 99 cents, but also € 1.99, € 2.99 and up. In the E-book market also many opportunities for alternative offers arise. As an example, Amazon has a program called Kindle Unlimited (for $ 9.99 unlimited 10 books on your reading shelf), the whole arsenal of commercial offerings are displayed: daily deals, monthly deals, 50 books for $ 2 per book, Kindle books to up to 65% discount, time-dependent price promotions, and so on. Innovation also takes place in sales offers.

Product form possibilities

Product form nowadays is more and more varied, for example by the preview capabilities of parts of the book, but also in the length of a story or text. The latter Dutch publisher WPG has tried several years ago with its Vertragingsapp. The reader could specify the time he wished to spend on a reading activity, by setting a clock. The app gave you options ranging from poetry, short stories or a portion of a book. Of course one also could order the book. The element of surprise for the reader is great, but in fact it also applies to editorially driven solutions such as Elly's Choice (by publisher VBK), where a fixed number of books is chosen by editors each month. By experimenting with these kind of innovative presentations there are possibilities to see where audiences feel comfortable with.

Cost allocation and solutions

It seems like a logical problem when it comes to price level and sales volume. Lower prices and more sales offers should lead to higher sales potential in a product-push market like the book market. In particular, the pricing mechanism should lead to less piracy, which hinders the current sales. That is actually the state of affairs where the world of the E-book in general is now.

The P-book has supported the E-book for long by absorbing all cost allocations. Apart from the distorted price development of an E-book that ensued (to win just as much as possible on an E-book, by charging everything to the P-book and by keeping the price of the E-book high), it is not a tenable model. If the number of E-books grow the publisher will be forced to do realistic cost allocations. I would advocate to take the development of a story including translation and editing as central costs and divide this over the - pre - estimated sales of the story in p or e form. In retrospect, a post calculation should make it clear whether the fees are properly distributed. It would prevent at least easily given discounts to E-books that will never compensate the fixed costs of creating the book.

Settlement of royalties for the author will have to go another way, too. I would like to adjust the model of a royalty percentage to a percentage of the transferprice of all of the physical and electronic forms in a sliding scale, rather than on the sales price. And if the author is not satisfied he can always take self publishing as an option: it is a high risk high-return model for the author, although it is clear that not every author is born as an entrepreneur.

[Benchmark]

"To measure everything doesn't make you happy, said the idealist. But measuring nothing keeps you poor, said the analist."

Anonymus

Waste lurks around the corner at publishing, as already described in earlier chapters. That waste hinders the bookindustry enormously. It is clear that the entrenched relationships in the bookindustry limit the mobility of publishing, crisis or no crisis. And it is also clear that a different perspective is needed to look at publishing as such. I'll do this in the following chapters.

Firstly, numerical analyses of how publishers actually work is of interest. These analyses could provide more insight into how publishers do their job compared to each other.

In 2014 a benchmark was set up containing the basic cost and turnover figures for all books of 14 publishers. The figures for some cost parts are modeled by assumptions to arrive at comparable values in terms of profit per book title.

The results of the analyses from the benchmark are meant to contribute to and underline strategic alternatives for the book industry. As said before it seems as if a publisher is forced to publish only bestsellers, but in the chain of the publishing process, I'll give him a way out to practice the publsihing trade in a healthy, profitable and promising way.

Analysed costs in the benchmark

To make optimal comparisons in the benchmark all costs are included except overhead and margin. Earnings per edition in the Benchmark therefore represent the direct contribution (plus or minus) to the end result.

All contributions added together could indicate whether a publisher earns anything in theory or fails to pay for overhead (and profit). Needless to say that a part of all costs stem from modelled costs (see Appendix 2).

The costs are edited in such an anonymous and partly modeled way they can not be traced to actual publishers. They do project reality proportionally by title and as such the Benchmark is a good basis for comparison between publishers themselves and represents a view on the whole Dutch market.

Chapter 11

Analyses on numbers, revenues and costs

From 14 publishers numerical data were collected and where data failed (see Appendix 2 for some of the elements used) weighted assumptions were added. In the benchmark analysis it is attempted to clarify some specific industry practices surrounding the publishing of P-books. The sample covers a period of eighteen months, in which 5,000 titles were produced and published by the 14 publishers. Because it's not always about new titles, but also reprints (sometimes several within this period), re-releases and backlist titles by these same publishers, I looked at the underlying stories of these different ISBNs. So I came to over 2800 clustered titles (so sometimes multiple ISBNs for the same story).

I also looked at the revenue and the total cost per title, that is, I took the original story of the author and included all the reprints, reissues and other formats (hardcover, paperback, pocket, et cetera.) that have been issued in the relevant period. Therefore I looked at the profitability of the whole story; it boils down to the profitability of the whole story in all (currently: paper) formats.

Number of titles

The graph below shows how many titles these publishers produced in the measured period of eighteen months. There are big differences, but please note that these are all stories that have been issued in that period of eighteen months, including reissues and reprints etc.

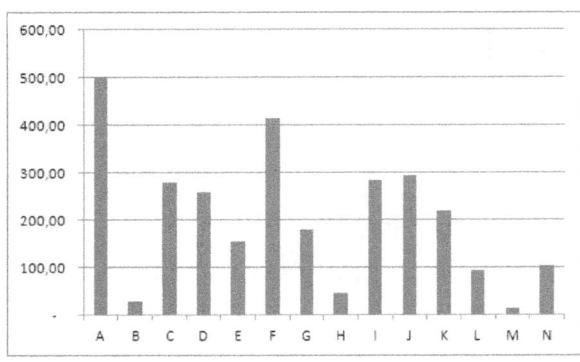

Fig. 11.1 Number of Titles perPublisher published during measurement period

To enter the waste-discussion around producing stories all titles are shown in terms of turnover and in terms of costs in an overview (see Fig. 11.2 and subsequent figures) where vertically sales turnover is shown and horizontally costs (also compare Elberse, *Blockbusters* , p. 42). In addition, there is a line drawn from lower left to upper right. This line indicates where revenues and costs are equal, the break-even level. The principle is simple: if the title is above the line, then your title makes a gain, it's underneath, then your title makes a loss.

Revenues and costs

To get a better view of the results for each title every title from the benchmark database is represented in figure 11.2 by a bullet. Each dot represents a title in all its formats (hardcover, paperback, reprint, reissue, etc.) taken together. There is also a break-even line drawn to quickly get a feel at profit or loss per title. The total database will look as follows, assuming clustered titles (ie 2800 dots).

To get a good grasp on how crowded it is around the point where revenue-axis and cost-axis intersect, I can zoom in on one group, where titles make less than € 10,000 turnover and costs. It turns out that it contains 1179 titles and it is represented in figure 11.3.

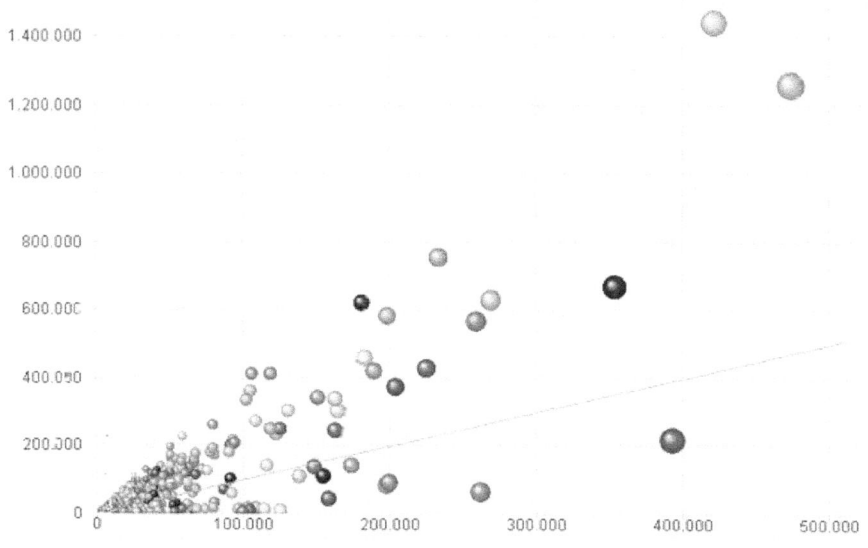

Fig. 11.2 Turnover-Cost-graph of the entire benchmark database (QlikView)

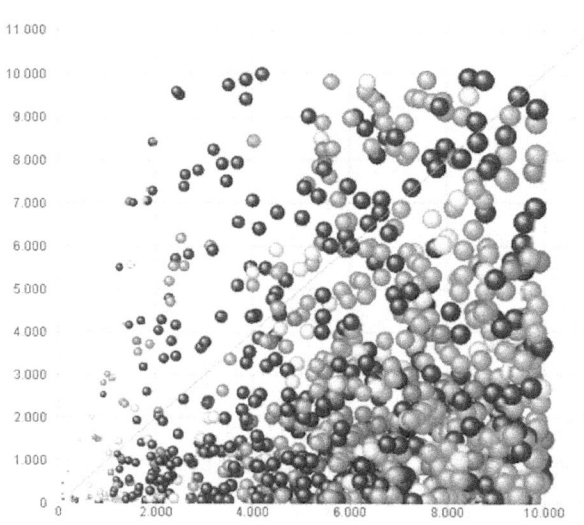

Fig. 11.3 Turnover-Cost graph of the benchmark database up to € 10,000
(QlikView)

The squares or clusters

For the analysis I chose (see Fig. 11.4) to make a classification of five different 'squares' or clusters of turnover size, coupled with a similar cost level, starting with a sales and cost of less than € 10,000, rising to € 60,000 and further. This is used to look at the database. The number of titles associated with these squares is shown in the schematic diagram in figure 11.4.

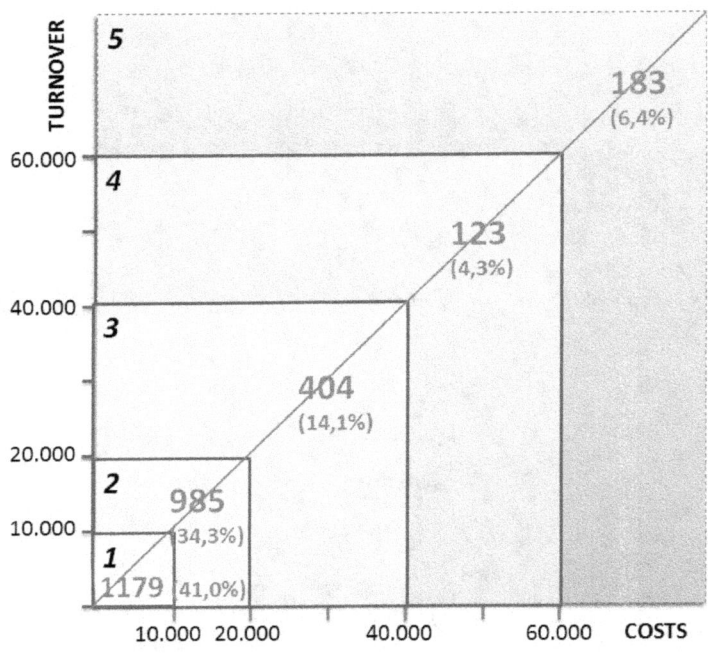

Fig. 11.4 Revenue Cost matrix with numbers of titles per cluster

The layout is deliberately chosen because the combination of cost and revenue within a certain cluster includes both the extreme wins and the extreme misses. For example, when a high turnover is scored with a low cost (which is incidentally not easy with a P-book because of production costs, but with an E-book it is quite conceivable) then you have the ultimate bestseller.

Conversely, if you chose to do a massive productionrun (high costs) because you expect a bestseller, but sales remains low, then I judge this title still to be in the segment where higher sales was expected.

As an example, the upper limit I have set as "more than € 60,000 turnover and costs". Which in this case means that 6.4% of the database, ie 183 title clusters, ended up in this cluster.

What is striking is that there are very many titles around the intersection of the lines of cost and revenue, and that the differences are very big with titles with higher sales. More than 75% of the titles make less than € 20,000 turnover and costs plus half of those titles falls into cluster 1, less than € 10,000.

In itself these figures don't tell much because they don't shed a light on profitability or capital investment, but what the numbers make clear is that publishers make a huge effort for these small titles (including management attention, resources, etc.)

Turnover, costs, margin

If I add up all fictitious turnover of all publishers together I arrive at the following breakdown over the whole measurement period:

Nearly 55% of sales are generated by, as we just saw, 183 (6.4%) of the number of titles. In short: the best sellers bring on the bulk of the turnover. Slightly less than 11% of the titles get nearly 65% of sales for these publishers. This turnover consists of titles from the cluster with € 40,000 onwards in sales and costs.

This is no Pareto distribution (the 20-80 rule) but it does seem like it. Almost 90% of the titles generates only 35% of the money and all attention will be on those titles.

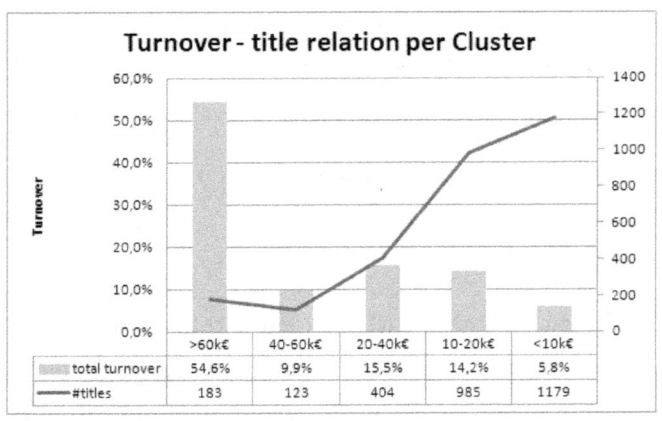

Fig. 11.5 Turnover per cluster of titles

In the more emotional debate within the bookindustry common knowledge has it that the top products finance the poorly performing products. If this judgment would be based on turnover only, then it's right, but: you must count the cost as well. And if you do, immediately the first inaccuracy of the statement becomes visible. If I add the total cost per cluster to the above figures, then it will look as follows.

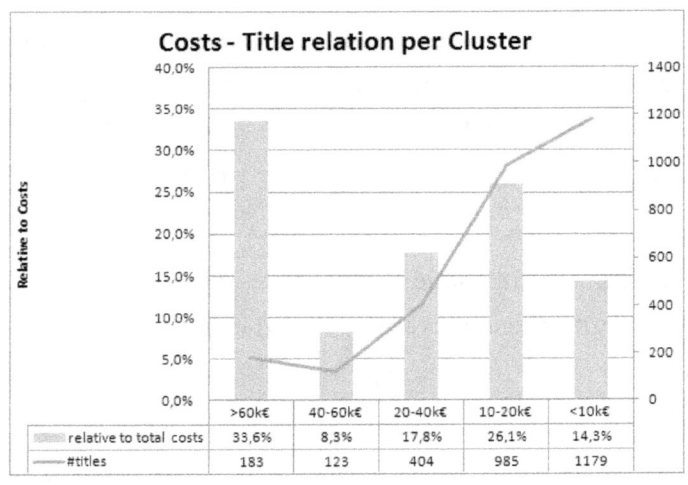

Fig. 11.6 Costs per cluster

The top 11% of the titles make 65% of revenue, but slightly more than 40% of the cost. But almost 90% of smaller titles generate 35% of sales by almost 60% of the cost. The amount of money that is trapped in the smaller titles is substantial. It is about half (between 40 and 60%) of the total capital spent on cost! But what really catches the eye is the resulting margin, ie the difference between revenue and costs, the contribution that the publisher delivers to cover for his overhead and profit.

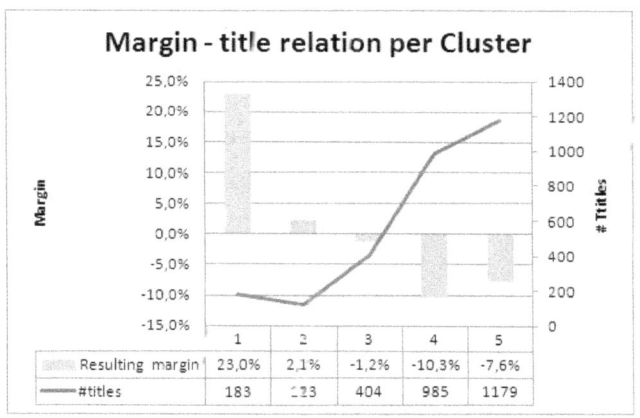

Fig11.7 Margin per cluster

This is the most remarkable 'flaw' in the system. The loss-making titles are being sponsored by some big profit makers. But the loss is so great that the entire industry is pulled down. The results further show that:

. If I added all publishers, they make about 5.9% margin together compared to the turnover. With this 5.9% the overhead and profit should still be paid. That's telling something about the profitability of the industry!

. Out of the benchmark of 14 publishers seven publishing houses made a loss even before deduction of overhead and profit.

This indicates that the cross-subsidization within a publishing house in at least half of the cases is no longer sufficient. The causes are primarily located in the aforementioned waste and the stalling strategic principles which have led to it. More about that later.

Loss making and profitable titles

The numbers are even more shocking when examining the results of loss-making (minus) and profitable works (plus) per each cluster: a division was created to see how much positive titles there are against loss-making projects. That should be an indication of how successful a particular segment is.The figure shows per cluster what the profitable titles contribute to margin (plus), calculated relative to the total turnover. And how the loss-making (minus) titles determine the result. The difference between the two determines the final margin. The third bar per cluster displays the resulting margin or contribution to overhead and profit. Which is added for all publishers across all clusters and results in 5.9% of sales.

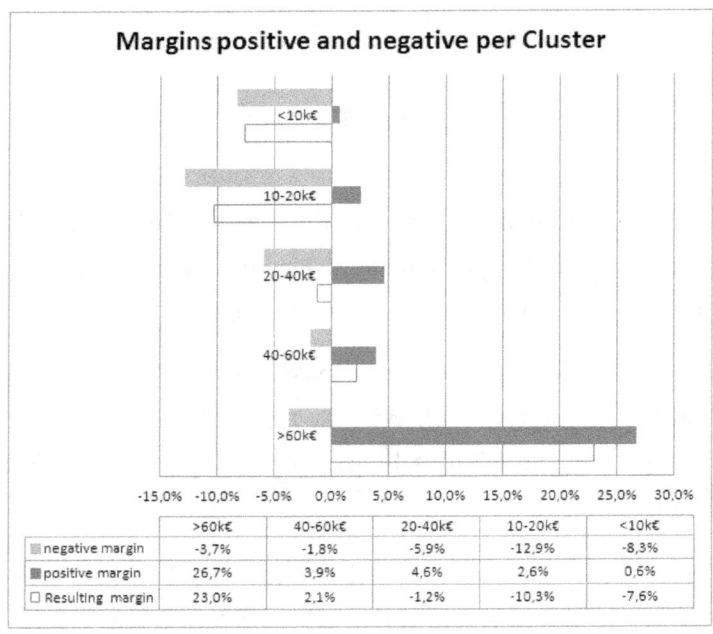

	>60k€	40-60k€	20-40k€	10-20k€	<10k€
negative margin	-3,7%	-1,8%	-5,9%	-12,9%	-8,3%
positive margin	26,7%	3,9%	4,6%	2,6%	0,6%
Resulting margin	23,0%	2,1%	-1,2%	-10,3%	-7,6%

Fig. 11.8 Margins per cluster of profitable and loss-making titles

It is undeniably true that for titles with small revenues and expenses the balance has a very negative deflection. Titles under € 10,000 are almost by definition a loss. They contribute for 0.6% of the total profit and for over 8% of all losses. But the next category (from € 10,000 to € 20,000), seems even worse: some 13% of the total revenue is loss making and only 3% helps the overall figure to a resulting 10% negative contribution. It improves as revenues and costs increase, but only with titles that score above the € 40,000 turnover/cost cluster the balance seems to restore in the right way. Naturally there are also numbers of titles that contribute negatively and thereby pull down the balance. Above € 60,000 you can see that some 4% of total revenue is a loss: hoped for bestsellers that didn't become one.

If you do the same calculations relatively per square, so if you look at the plus and minus per square, then it reels ones head altogether. The two smallest turnover clusters (up to € 20,000) create tens of percentpoints negative contribution and make it totally unattractive to invest money in there.

Obviously some issues are attributable to the assumptions made in the model for costs that were not directly measured, but overall trends and conclusions based on in this benchmark are well-founded indeed.

It is impossible that an industry with the above trends lasts long. The most poignant conclusion in this model is that on closer inspection the titles under € 20,000 cannot exist in the current way of creation, production and promotion.

The big titles are much more profitable in absolute terms and the loss-makers do not necessarily lose much more. The turning point is at around € 40,000, where break-even occurs. Of course it seems interesting to avoid anything that is 'minus'; A new strategy will have to do everything it can to get it into proportion. The total avoidance of loss-making products is an illusion, but to realize a real ratio between winners and losers should be possible.

A slightly different view of the financial affairs is shown in the figure below, in which the main elements are weighed against the average number of titles.

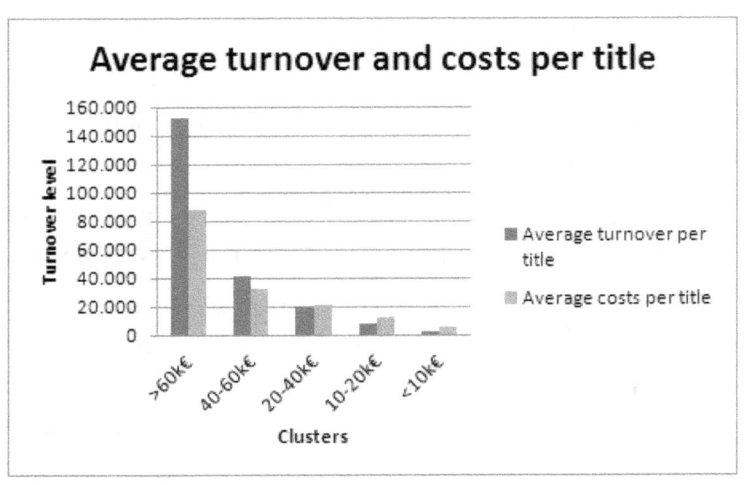

Fig. 11.9 Average revenues and costs per title

At quick glance small titles seem to be the culprits, because making a book easily costs between € 5,000 to € 10,000 in the present structure. But if you look longer and better, you have to qualify that opinion, because the average cost of a bestseller and the distribution among the various cost elements also require a strategic review. Since all the figures are totaled and are on average, they do not say anything about the underlying nature: there are for example cross-sections to be made on theme, for example, on the basis of NUR, or on the basis of the underlying publishing company, or on the basis of the type of edition (pocket or hard cover for example), even on the basis of the author, and so on.

Chapter 12

Causes and lessons

To analyse why publishers on the whole have bad margins, I looked in our research to the previously discussed cost elements, successively.

Royalties: to get a similar starting point in the benchmark the model assumed equivalent royalties per author. In practice this is not evident from the ever-increasing advances paid to established writers and in particular to authors of bestsellers. That should reduce the margins of bestseller titles and that is probably what happens in practice. Here I can only say that royalties are not distinctive enough to draw conclusions.

Translation costs: The costs of translation are included as standard in the benchmark model and also on the basis of these costs few conclusions are to be made. A translated work may be more costly in the final analysis because there is an extra cost in addition to a royalty arrangement for the author's. The figure below illustrates this. The distribution over the various publishers points out - except that there are seven profitable and seven loss-making parties - margin contributions by foreign translated works are quite different. That also applies to the Dutch titles, but even more it is a prelude to the discussion on focus in the next chapter.

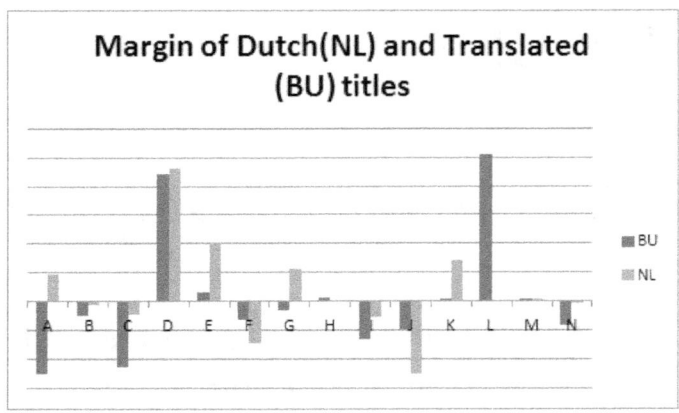

Fig. 12.1 Margin contribution per publisher of translated Dutch (NL) and foreign (BU) titles

Editing. Again, the model gives no answer, other than that it is assumed that only one revision round is used per a book. In practice there are often much more revision rounds, bringing additional costs including personnel and that in turn is diminishing the margin (contribution to overhead and profit). I reiterate standardisation opportunities, not very popular in publishing, but a sure way to go to achieve solid gains. This standardisation applies mutatis mutandis to typesetting and finishing.

Production costs. Here profitable publishers act smarter than the loss-making. Often the more profitable ones act a factor of 3 to 4 more efficient, plan much better and manage their (smallest possible) stock better. Nevertheless much more (profit) can be achieved as a result of operating in a strategically sound way. Also, one can quickly see that at the lower end of the spectrum still too much is produced in relation to sales numbers.

Promotion. It is difficult to determine what is distinctive because no predominant pattern in marketing spend can be found. The publishers in general spend about the same, percentagewise.

Moreover, it is also impossible to determine how the money is spent and with what degree of spread over media. And finally it is unknown what audiences are reached best with the euros spent for marketing communications.

What the numbers do say is that the moment has come to pose some important strategic questions to improve the structure issue around improving publishing, renewing it and transforming it too. Too much is produced at the lower regions of publishing, which creates onerous waste. In addition, the capital requirement is out of proportion. This waste suffocates the industry. The questions I want to ask are:

1 What are the ways to stop waste?

2 What are the possibilities for increasing the 'success rate' of a book?

3 To survive, you can invest in innovation. What steps are needed to do more innovation and in what areas?

In the following chapters I answer these questions, and give solutions to provide publishing with a new perspective.

[Strategy]

"When I was tired of searching, I learned to find."

Friedrich Nietzsche

Before you consider a strategy, you should ask yourself the question: why am I here? And for whom? In the publishing industry it means for the latter, of course: the customer, the reader, the consumer of a narrative experience.

This requires a discussion about audiences, the needs that you want to accommodate for those target groups and the efforts and capital requirement to provide it. In my conclusions about marketing and marketing efforts it has become clear that the average publisher does not operate on 'fact-based' marketing. It often goes by gut-feel or authority (of an author or publisher or the editor).

Chapter 13

Instinctive feeling, luck and publishing

The lack of a clear strategic focus on audiences and customer gratification makes that factors of luck and instinct are excessively present in publishing. Objectively speaking this non-focus on audiences is damaging and success patterns around bestsellers and the general lack of success in copycat competitors are proof that luck is absolutely no merit and no guarantee for the next bestseller either. I am under the strong impression that the publishing world clings passionately to the myth that a publishers instinct is the reason when it comes to success and it is the fault of the market when it comes to failure.

This myth is disastrous or in other words, much of the publishing world is in denial when it comes to the acceptance of fact-based marketing to support the development of reader behavior and innovations based on that reader behaviour.

Everyone knows the story of J. K. Rowling, author of the *Harry Potter* series, who was constantly rejected by publishers. And that years after her resounding success with the *Harry Potter* series her adult novels, written under a pseudonym, generated but moderate sales.

Was that because of the publishers? Or of the readers? Why could the publisher not continue Rowling's previous successes with her novels for adults? Was it lack of instinct?

Some other examples. For the publisher of *Fifty shades of Gray* it seemed as if a new audience had stood up, but his competitors who eagerly wanted to get a piece of the pie by selling similar literature, could not match that success by far. The success of Dan Brown holds exactly the same argument.

Why was a book like *Stoner* in the 60s a modest success and in the 21st century suddenly a bestselling title? Would that have been the case in , say, as the 80s, or 90s? Was it a deliberate plan or 'just a streak of luck '?

Why are some publishers successful during a certain period and then not for years? Did they just lose it? Or do they have just a little less luck?

Explanations

It is interesting to see how unsuccessful publishing is explained. The explanations are rarely accompanied by relevant statistics to support the declared argument. What it boils down to is that everyone who asserts something is automatically right. The opposite can not be proven. And if such closed reasoning is the case, then in my opinion luck must be in play.

In itself, my reasoning is very generalising: for example, there will always be commercial skill and knowledge needed to entice people to buy a story. And this want making, which we recognise from the advertising world and the world of marketing, is partly based on statistical reasoning and partly on luck.

My plea is therefore to give greater recognition to these two factors ('fact-based marketing' and 'luck') and to give a greater role to the figures and analyses that go with them. In the online world it is no question anymore but a necessity altogether. There every step that is taken in a single process is supported by big data analyses.

Case: Predicting a bestseller

The belief in the more numerical approach to publishing is in my opinion the real challenge for the field. Whether the community of publishers, authors, editors, retailers etc. will join in too remains to be seen but there are already many initiatives that aim to reduce the luck factor and want to do more objectified statements about the success of a story. Can a publisher predict a bestseller? The answer is 'not yet', but a number of trends suggest that that possibility quickly approaches.

In *Success with Style: Using Writing Style to Predict the Success of novels* a number of researchers at Stony Brook University describe the ability to analyse features of writing style and thus to recognise the characteristics of successful commercial books. 'Stylometry' is the science that focuses on the language aspects of a story (and author) features, such as length of sentences and words and the frequency of certain words. This knowledge helped among other things to expose JK Rowling as the author for a novel written under pseudonym. James S. Murphy goes one step further in *When will machines start predicting bestsellers?*, in which he makes clear that the foundation has already been laid for the automated prediction of successful books. The University of Amsterdam is researching these types of analysis as a prelude to computer-assisted predictions.

Because companies like Amazon and Apple have incredible insight through their database of customer and behavioral data and are therefore particularly well able to do predictions, it is still only a few steps further away to create publishing strategies based on new texts supplied and therefore to attack the 'slushpile' with computer aided techniques. The publisher gets help in this way.

Apple may serve as an illustration. It recently bought BOOKlamp, an environment where on the basis of data analyses on existing titles it tries to extract data on all sorts of variables and makes predictions from it. The accuracy is sometimes frightfully good. But the scientists themselves know that the success of a book depend on so many more factors: marketing, promotion, TV broadcasts and the spot on the bestseller list itself. And of course, in part, also the factor of luck or chance. There will always be room for the enthusiasm and knowledge of a publisher but lots of selection factors will also come from machines in the future.

Even if big data analytics lead to only a 50% probability to predict the success of a story, the result will always be better compared to how a publisher currently scores in his efforts to sell stories successfully and profitably. A small calculation shows that the current deficit incurred on the badseller part of our benchmark wil turn into a profitable operation when big data analytics are deployed. It has no sense to shrug or to deny the developments; the least a publisher can do is to start collecting data on the customer, customer behavior and customer preferences.

A caveat here: blindly following big data adepts who claim that in this way luck becomes a choice, goes too far. This kind of improvement I suggest can be reached by great efforts and investments (and consequently focus on numerical approach and the use of big data), but luck is never a certainty. Sometimes you have to have the courage to admit that chance has given a helping hand.

Chapter 14

Three questions as a basis for new strategies

The three questions posed at the end of chapter 12 are essentially questions that want to solve three issues in the publishing world:

1. How can you stop the waste?

2. How do you create the opportunity to increase the success rate of a book?

3. How can you innovate - especially if the waste is stopped ?

Later I work out the details, but in short you can summarize the answers as follows:

. Waste is stopped through focus in everything you do and by saving costs in your publishing process.

. The success rate of a book increases by focusing on target group, theme, in short: in marketing with a capital M.

. And innovation is the result when there is money left - thanks to your earlier emphasis on focus at the first two points - to start initiatives yourself or with other (cooperation or acquisition) parties.

Appendix 1 shows what the underlying strategic framework contains on which we base this chapter.

The first question 'how to stop the waste', is also the toughest: the benchmark shows that 40 to 60% of the costs and thus the capital requirement of a publishing house is put in badsellers. Securing some 50% of your capital in high risk with an average negative return of about 10% (!) is not wise, while a bestseller gives a yield of approximately 23%. Not many people will invest their savings in that way and the comparison with a Casino is easily made here: you constantly put half of your chips on the wrong color, and the payoff of the other half is unfavorable, too.

The other aspects of the cost make the question even more unfavorable: the entire company, every employee spends half of his time on producing and contributing to waste. Each new title that you publish is a bet of at least € 10,000 again on red or black. € 10,000 spent on reading and reading reports, translation costs and editing efforts, production, discussions on the cover, layout, paper, promotion, etcetera. And because the chances are that the book does not sell well expensive storage costs are added. But also in the back office, where people are busy getting the title in a catalog, where sales people in turn with a suitcase full of titles have to persuade the bookshops and distributors. This is about the almost devastating amount of dispersion of attention.

Remedy: more focus

The remedy is obvious: produce titles, try to deal more efficiently with editorial effort (less text revisions), make more standardised books, both in form and layout, smarter ways for print run determination, smaller catalogs for sales, et cetera. In short: more focus.

Everyone can rationalise and economise, but that doesn't always help a company forward. In practice after rationalisations one returns to old habits simply by acquiring and producing titles the old way. Partly because it seems like the demand for reading books is dropping and also - and that is an economic rule - because not so many large profits are made, one is almost forced to adopt a classic market share strategy.

In short this means that one is trying to capture the largest possible market share; usually that means by investing extra promotion for the product (the titles) and the brand (the publisher). In that way one is trying to steal share of its competitor. It means to sacrifice margin per product because a lot of money is spent on promotion and brand development. The theory is that it pays off to generate more attention to the product and in this case more of the product is sold and thus one still can make a reasonable profit.

Another measure is usually: acquisitions (read: buying market share) and the concentration of activities to keep overhead costs low in order to earn enough money. Thus in the Netherlands, WPG and Lannoo / Meulenhoff in recent decades, grew by buying other publishers. This particular model has also had its best time again; These days for instance cooperation conglomerates arise working with the same principles of concentration and market share, but without the large acquisition payments, such as Overamstel Publishers (formerly Dutch Media Publishers) and VBK Publishers. Perhaps these cooperation conglomerates also arise because there is less risk capital left to finance large acquisitions (see also the case description in chapter 2).

Visibility of publishers

I was talking about market share strategy, but that also asks for brand awareness. How strong is the brand and how much pressure is there on publishers to be visible?

Let's start with the readers: brand does not matter, it is about the author. The brand of the publisher doesn't say much to readers.

Then the author: in most cases he is not very picky about publishers. Because there has always been a huge supply of manuscripts, authors are more than happy when a publisher is willing to publish his or her book. So there is no excessive pressure to be distinctive as a publisher. On the other hand from the publishers point of view there is a need to be distinctive in the sales channel, because of the overwhelming supply from publishers there is a huge fight for shelf space with distributors.

Yet that battle has not led to clear profiles of publishers. It is my perception that the cycle of offer catalogs (usually three times a year) gives a massive burden with many publishers and for buyers a kind of resignation because they can not properly evaluate all offers simply through lack of time. Every year there are thousands of titles and judging all of them is simply impossible.

Three elements that help focus

In my opinion the constant shrinking and crumbling of the publishing industry can be prevented only by using three structural elements, and then choose from three strategies. Those three elements are:

Element 1: Choose a focus on a publishing theme

Element 2: Choose a targetgroup

Element 3: Innovate with solutions to customer needs

Below I will discuss each of these three elements.

Element 1: Choose a focus on a publishing theme

The publishing industry is an opportunistic industry, and that is understandable if you are basically operating from out of the casino. It means that a publisher continually reacts to opportunities and chances to publish a story on a topic that appeals to him. And with which he as an entrepreneur hopes to earn money. To let go of this expediency is of the utmost importance for the strategies we are about to develop.

After all, without focus on choosing a publishing theme you can never build a brand. Why would an author award his work to you as a publisher if you have absolutely nothing with his theme? How can you efficiently access readers if you do not know what triggers them on that theme? How can you excite a distributor to sell your books if you do not focus on that topic?

More importantly the question is: do you want to be one of the best brands on said topic so you can dominate that market or at least be an influential player?

These are quite normal questions to ask entrepreneurs in any industry and especially for companies that offer more online oriented products and services. Sadly in the publishing world the mantra is 'choosing is losing' and that's the reason why nothing really changes. Precisely my opinion is that not choosing is losing - reflected in all the figures which have been shown so far.

Case: NUR-codes as theme

A theme is a subject on which the publisher wants to distinguish himself. In the Netherlands for this purpose we have NUR-codes.

This coding of themes within the book trade in the Netherlands is not unique but - although the definitions for NUR code leave room for interpretation - usable. NUR stands for Dutch Uniform Classification and is a three-digit code. The main codes are listed in the table below, which can in turn be divided in subcodes. For examples the figure 3 can be subdivided in 300, 310 up to 370, and is again per ten further subdivided.

For example 300 is divided into 301 (literary novel / novella) to 309 (anthology), and 310 (pockets general) is divided by 311 (pockets literary fiction) to 315 (translated pockets).

NUR main code	Description main code
000	Non-books
100	Educational books
200	Children's books
300	Literary fiction
400	Non-fiction leisure
500	Travel
600	Non-fiction informative/professional
700	Theology
800	Business
900	Social geography

Fig. 14.1 List with main NUR-codes

So there is considerable differentiation in detail in terms of theme. And because of this diversity, there is room for creative shuffling.

The quality and accuracy of the choice of a NUR code leaves much to be desired. The strength of the NUR codes themselves is therefore questionable and the lack of an objective alternative is strongly felt.Reportedly NUR codes are especially chosen so a book can sit on the right table in a bookstore, and therewith contamination has occurred in the reliability of the resulting data. This makes it difficult to produce reliable analyses based on NUR codes, but as said before unfortunately currently nothing better is at hand.

Illustrative are the sheer number of NUR codes on which a publisher publishes. Its quantity endorse the argument that focussing on a few themes is not yet very widespread. Only one publisher from the benchmark has limited himself to a single NUR code, the rest uses at least 10.

What is striking is that the profitability of a publisher correlates with the number of NUR codes that he publishes in: the seven loss-making publishers have on average 23 NUR codes where the profitable publishers have used 12. Focus on this area would therefore (also) have to help.

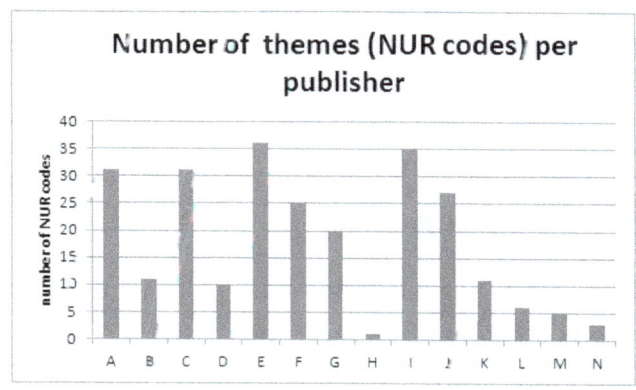

Fig. 14.2 number of NUR codes per publisher in the Benchmark

I am convinced that concentration and focus on themes and associated groups will pay out eventually. This means that investments are necessary in marketing, customer behavior and resources to both analyse and develop the customer behavior.

Choosing, evaluating and adjusting a theme is not a small operation. But it is important to choose a theme. Period.

Element 2: Choose a targetgroup

As has been previously mentioned, the choice of target groups that are connected to the publishing themes is of importance to know what portfolio of books and services need to be developed and offered.

I've talked before about persona, example types of customers who are described by what they do and what they want. Persona investigation in the Netherlands has been done by NOM or Motivaction to mention a few and serve as possible input for the targeting and the development of the portfolio.

Collecting customer information is traditionally done at the bookstore and by research agencies such as GfK, who have been previously instructed by the publisher association NUV to coordinate this. The data consists mainly of cash register data and is sometimes extended and enhanced by panelgroup interviews. The bookstore has very limited tools to get information on who buys books and why. Which is why cash-register information hitherto always was the main source of data. The online distribution parties on the contrary have this information in abundance but are not willing to share it with publishers or retailers.

Research on customers

Research on customer buying habits and reading habits to my knowledge have never been done on a large scale in the Netherlands; libraries have done a few investigations, but always with a focus on lending books.

It should be second nature to publishers to base all acts performed around making books from distilling knowledge about readers and their reading habits. You bet that Amazon and Bol.com indeed are doing exactly that.

My experience is that the current generation of publishers is not numerically driven. Publishers are usually people who have a background in the humanities and have no empathy for numbers.

The challenge is to provide this group of people, who still make the publishing decisions, with something to make an easy connection between content and figures. Not an easy task and it will take some time.

Case: customer research

The British publisher Random House is trying to set a good example through their Customer Insights Team. The team is in fact a group trying to deliver context at (marketing) figures.

Marketers are usually those trained in the social sciences (psychology, etc.), and it is their task to build a bridge between the more emotionally driven publishers and the numerically and technically driven managers and ICT specialists.The team has chosen to include panels of thousands of enthusiastic readers questioning them regularly with questionnaires and interviews.

The results are always instructive and useful. So the team for example indicates that research on behavior showed that readers feel that they are well informed about books that matter, but that choosing the next book is a major barrier. Based on that a publisher can tune efforts and titles to that identified problem.

Another practical example is that they found out that thrillers rarely end up on the bookshelf of the reader. The book is passed on to someone else or simply thrown away. Often there are heated discussions within publishing companies whether a book would look good in the bookcase, and there are long discussions about the quality of typesetting, paper and cover; that energy can be used effectively with these insights, and thus help reduce the waste.

Publishers would be well advised to embrace targeting customer groups and (permanent) research into the behavior and attitudes of their customers.

Element 3: Innovate with solutions to customer needs

You as an entrepreneur can make a P-book or E-book for a reading experience, but as we have seen, the consumer demand is often much more variable than just 'I want a book'. From my analysis one can also delve into questions like: where, at what place does the customer want to read a book (a distribution issue)? Does he want to have more choice of titles (also a distribution question)? Does he want more background to the story (more content)? Or books with a similar theme to the story (even more content)?

Is it any wonder that the publishing industry has been caught up by start-ups? The functionality a reader requires does not necessarily stop at the story itself. The context is just as important and that is why initiatives such as Scribd and Oyster have arrived, who opted for streaming solutions where the respective group of readers has unlimited choice, convenience of payment and availability everywhere. The solutions are already underway in dozens of countries (Scribd) so that the initiatives in Europe (Skoobe) look rather poorly in that respect.

Rights issues also hinder these initiatives, especially in Europe, where local laws and regulations on copyright also create difficult situations. With payment and subscription models new entrants experiment widely, but it is expected that it will also rapidly crystallize.

What's even more interesting, these initiatives automatically create platforms of self publishing. Scribd allows documents, reports, but also music and books (!) to be uploaded and shared or just to be sold at a fee. In this way the role of the publisher continues towards the development of features and capabilities for readers, something publishers for professionals and science are doing already for years.

Amazon also focuses on the development of capabilities and opportunities for the reader, but from the distribution side: Amazon has a self-publishing platform, Kindle Direct Publishing, and has been market leader for a considerable number of years in the English-speaking market.

In the Netherlands a self publishing initiative from a publisher started, Brave New Books. This is an initiative of Singel Publishers, Bol.com and Mybestseller.com. It is within the scope of this book too far for a complete inventory, but the opportunities for publishers are almost unlimited. Only hardly anyone seems to realize that these opportunities are serious.

Building skill sets with today's publishers and creating structured innovation takes time and that is the problem right now. The positioning of publishers around streaming in the Netherlands is illustrative. The CB has anticipated for the entire industry by creating an E-book distribution environment, but the initiatives developed around it by publishers are either limited in options (VBK) or are delayed (Lannoo / WPG). It is even so that libraries are far ahead of most publishers when it comes to offering E-books (Bibliotheek.nl). Publishers are still too afraid that channel conflicts arise, or hassles with authors rights issues. Problems enough but still no one has risen from the publishing ranks to stimulate a breakthrough.

Conclusion

Cutting costs is traditionally a prerequisite for every good strategy and not an end in itself, but something that must be pursued diligently and continuously.

In the creation process less correction cycles should be sought after, and serious consideration should be given to what editorial layers can be outsourced instead of keeping everything within the publishing house. At production level, room must be made for intelligent circulation and print run policies and procurement opportunities; storage should be avoided and controlled by the same clever production environments; the marketing department must be given more weight and be reinforced with marketing intelligence; and overhead should be reduced, if this is at least not at the expense of innovation. Then the publisher should focus more clearly: what is our theme, what our audiences what our customer needs?

Based on that we can choose a strategy: how do we handle all of this?

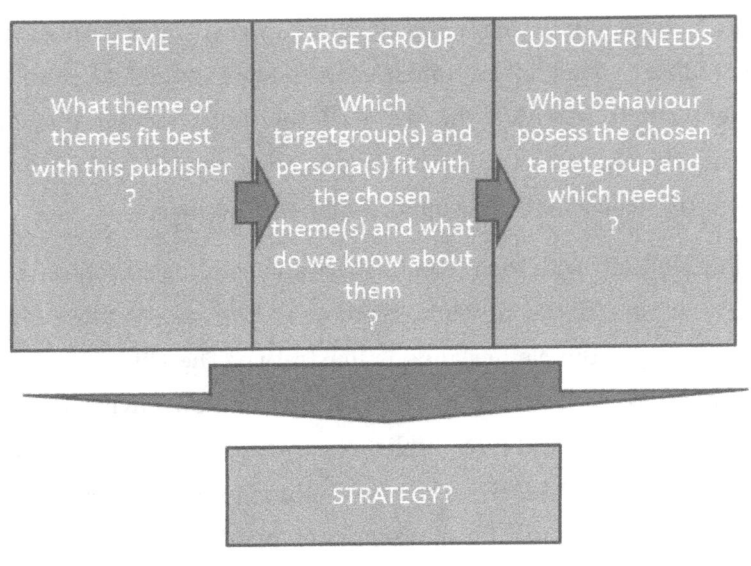

Fig. 14.3 Three strategic elements as the basis for a new strategy

Chapter 15

A new strategy

Strategy is to determine how you reach your goal. The goal is clear: no more betting too much money on red or black and stopping all waste. And besides, the purpose is to be able to spend the amount of capital of the publisher on the successes and (real) innovation in such a manner that the publisher can fully participate in the battle for customers.

At this point it is interesting to take some elements from the book of Elberse. In her book *Blockbusters* she describes that for example in the film industry the major manufacturers do a limited amount of projects per year but allocate all their capital not only to production, but also to promotion and distribution. They thereby achieve good scores confirming Elberses theory of 'winner takes all'. The biggest turnovers come from this limited amount of movies. It yields so much money that it can support enough budget / capital for the next round.

The amount of failures is low and the yield of the successful films cover these. Innovation is rarely done, new filmmakers are not 'bred' only stars are recruited at fabulous salaries. The stars must create the large income because of their fame and proven success, such is the unwritten law.

Shifting talent

How do you create a movement that generates new talent and new stars? In essence it is the role of independent producers who admittedly operate at a greater risk factor, but spend correspondingly less budget.

Elberse describes in the case of the music industry even a real cooperation between the blockbuster music labels and the 'middle publisher'-producers: if a talent is discovered in the 'middlepublisher' then there are commitments that with certain turnover the band is adopted and taken over by the blockbuster publisher, with all the extra promotional budgets and attention that go with it.

The middle publisher continues to participate in the successes achieved by the respective band with the blockbuster publisher.

There is a form of 'breeding' by specialist producers, and an intelligent and accountable way to transfer the potential stars to the star producers. Similar systems are also seen in the entertainment industry like football where talents are spotted in the minor leagues and can continue to grow. The home-grown talent from educational institutions of particular soccer clubs also leads to a talent flow to the clubs.

The model

How does such a model work for publishers and is this model the answer to the three main questions we asked ourselves?

It shows from all our investigated possibilities and studies that a model with more focus on target groups, themes and client needs fits particularly well to a multi-layered model. Hence, we formulate the following three-tier model for publishing general books, coupled with the 'squares' or clusters which we have come across in the benchmark:

.The Bestseller publisher

.The Middle publisher

.The Selfpublishing publisher

Let me first describe the characteristics of these three types of publishing.

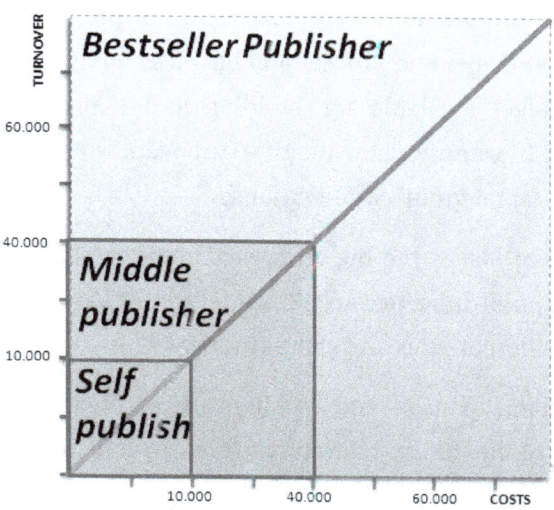

Fig. 15.1. The three-tier strategy for the publisher

The Bestseller publisher

Let me start by analogy with the book of Elberse with the bestseller publishing house, which has a 'winner takes all' strategy. This publisher has a limited number of titles and star authors in his portfolio. There is strong bidding on rights that are tendered on proven (foreign) authors and titles, and there are huge funds to acquire the titles. High advances, royalties and high budgets for marketing and promotion are available and the print runs of books are always high to very high.

The selection is fierce and nothing is left to chance when it comes to the target group determination and communication strategy. The losses may be big too but the potential profits are in principle higher. Margins do not even have to be very high, but the volume of money received from the margin per book is at a maximum.

That money is important for the next round of procurement of titles and stars. But a part is also spent on process and business innovation. There is always a considerable budget available for building and maintaining databases of customer behavior. It examines how the titles are read, who reads them and what are the best theme-target group combinations.

This intelligence makes the big difference between the bestseller publisher and other forms of publishing, because this intelligence has an important voice in the choice and selection of titles and star authors.

On the other hand sponsors and suppliers are targeted for an additional cash flow that the reach of the title and the star author can generate.

Within the bestseller publisher little is done to autonomous development of techniques and the like. However, much money is invested in the adoption of already developed and proven initiatives and companies.

The Middle publisher

The middle publisher looks like the publishing house as we know it: compared to the bestseller publisher a little more is invested in relatively unknown authors and writers not yet promoted to stardom. But unlike now the middle publisher mainly acquires writers and titles that have already proven to have a certain size in readership (like followers on Facebook). There is more strict control on theme and target audience than is usually now the case in publishing. Time is invested in the establishment of the brand, which must above all be consistent with the target market and (potential) authors.

Here, too, marketing intelligence is a mature part of the publishing activity and is used extensively in the title selection and buying of rights. Marketing and promotional efforts have a full budget and are excercised in the most modern way. No extreme amounts are offered for rights and authors such as with the bestseller publisher. Bestsellers are not the aim of this publishing house, but a steady stream of positively selling titles.

Innovation happens especially in the publishing process itself: marketing, distribution, target groups, reading habits and the like, and in some cases there is investment in self-publishing publishers, as we explain below. Authors are partly recruited from the transfers from selfpublishers; others are transferred from the middle publisher to bestseller publishers. Part of the business model is, therefore, that there is a flow of income from the bestseller publishers to this type of publisher.

The Selfpublishing publisher

At the bottom of the market, where the large number of serious writers and wannabes jostle each other, there is the self publishing environment. In the Netherlands alone there are, according to various estimates, between 700,000 to one million people writing a book. There is an industry emerging whereby the prospective author purchases services from a publisher (such as editing his manuscript) instead of receiving an advance.

Here authors can publish their work themselves at cost, with the support of editors, marketers, distribution specialists, cover designers, sales specialists and so on. The platforms that help these authors arose from all parts of the book chain. Sometimes they are distributors like Amazon, which offers one of the very first complete platforms for self publishing authors. But also publishers support this (such as Brave New Books in the Netherlands) and even printing companies participate in such initiatives. The latter are strongly driven to fill their machinery.

A service publisher will be an intermediary for the aforementioned specialties at this level and also provide a quality environment for aspiring authors. To be distinctive to the authors who are customers of the brand a strong focus on theme and target audiences is paramount. The specialty of the self-publishing publishing house thus becomes its business card. The brand of a self publishing publisher will therefore be very important.

The publishing houses will now have to show their true colors when it comes to their brand and image, so that the client (the author) may ask himself the question: 'Do I as a novice thriller writer want to be supported by an editor or a marketer who earns his money in nonfiction?' or 'Do I as a writer of historical novels feel comfortable with a marketer of poetry?'. The publisher in turn will want to keep an eye on where the potential selling authors are. Everything starts with focus on the right themes and the right audiences that the respective author endeavours to reach.

Reach as goal in itself

Let it be clear that the self-publishing publisher is also an answer to the big losses currently suffered with yet unproven authors and titles: for publishing a book a publisher can provide services with which it earns money (at least margin neutral) instead of which making significant losses. And also the self-publishing publisher reflects the great need of authors to get a better grip on the publishing of their own product. Dissatisfaction with current authors is mostly about the limited promotional attention that his publisher has to distribute among (too much) titles.

Participating in such a self-publishing platform, or with other initiatives such as lending of books and other mostly online streaming solutions for publishers, has more than one objective:

reach - creating scope for authors and readers, i.e. relevant numbers of customers, users and visitors

early warning and scouting - to be able to detect and track successful (self-publishing) authors and to scout them for - especially - the mid publisher

learn - collecting data in an environment where publishers and the entire supply chain can learn permanently. Because it is (often) about publishing E-books, this also is a way to gather data about reading habits of buyers but also about new distribution and promotion opportunities

business model- the way to establish a book at the very beginning of the chain in such a way that it makes money instead of it costing money

This model thus provides a picture of three kinds of publishers. each with their own characteristics and environments.

Chapter 16

Characteristics of the three types of publishers

The characteristics of the three types of publishers are summarized in the table below.

Characteristics (for NL)	Selfpublishing publisher	Middle publisher	Bestseller publisher
number of authors	very many	many dozens	dozens
turnover (transferprice) per title in €	max € 10,000	€ 10,000 - € 40,000	above € 40,000
number of readers	large individual reach	average	big
number of publishers	some (plus a great many small suppliers)	dozens	some
margin per publishertype	0% - 5%	10% - 15%	15%+
innovationbudgets/ warchest takeovers	5% - 10% of turnover	5% of turnover	10% of turnover

Fig. 16.1. Features of the three types of publishers

Number of titles and authors

It is clear that large amounts of titles and authors will be collected at the self publishers and with publishers that focus on these services. Very many authors will not rise above the level of self-publishing, and only a few dozen authors will thereafter move towards the first division (the middle publisher).

Only a handful of authors will arrive at the bestseller publisher. Please remind that 30% of books sold in the Netherlands is originally Dutch. Self publishing is about the Dutch authors, but the middle and bestseller publishers will have on average only 30% Dutch authors in their portfolios, the rest will be translated. That is already the case now (see Chapter 1, Figure 1.3.), so it will remain difficult for Dutch authors to advance to the middle publisher and beyond. It is expected, however, that more talent will be discovered through self publishing publishers than is the case up till. That's the reason that the 30% Dutch books in publishers portfolios will rise.

The € 10,000 limit we discussed earlier is the lower threshold at which the middle publishers will get their authors. For self-publishing authors € 10,000 is logically the upper limit. The limit to move on to the bestseller publisher will of course vary by country, but for the Netherlands I put it conveniently at € 40,000 turnover (transfer price) (which is a market turnover of approximately € 80,000). That also has to do with the ever increasing advances and contract terms with which manuscripts are acquired. It is the prerequisite of the bestseller publisher: they literally buy their security.

Number of readers

Depending on how the self publishing environment is positioned this branch will in particular draw large numbers of readers.for online purchases. The reach model that many (American) self publishers adhere to creates large amounts of readers and repeat visits by that group. It's because of the combination of selfpublishing- and shopping.

The pricing of E-books in this environment is a lot lower and immediately represents the value that can be tied to a story. Because the author has no track record, and perhaps not so many followers, the economic value is low. Due to all efforts by himself it will show later on whether his economic value may be higher. I think this is an important factor for the new industry of publishing. The P of Price in the marketing mix has a normal role as opposed to the regular bookmarket as we know it and rates will vary considerably.

For the middle publisher it is something else because in this environment all is realized in an almost classical manner and offered through all available channels. It will really depend on how middle publishing will further develop. Because all small, unknown and starting authors in this publishing house will no longer be published there will be a de facto different readership for this publisher, but by larger print runs of the titles its reach will be of high quality and well profiled. Price propositions will be more differentiated in proportion to the importance of the author and the theme. Especially if the fixed book price in the Netherlands is released.

The bestseller publishers will have a wide reach, because all the big sellers will be published by them. It will be interesting to see if and how bestseller publishers will be able to claim a specific thematic audience or that they will be still targeting a wide and general audience. Thrillers have always been a good selling genre. In the Netherlands, A. W. Bruna is a publishing house that profiles itself as a thriller publisher. It publishes the Black Bears series and major foreign thriller writers are bought, but yet it has no dominant position; there are many more publishers who have thrillers as bestselling titles. It is the challenge whether the large budgets that are necessary for this kind of editing, continue to be present in order to be and remain a bestseller publisher, even now as AW Bruna is part of the larger WPG Group.

Number of publishers in the three types

As indicated earlier, there are currently about 1,000 publishers in the Dutch market. Because of the crisis since 2009 dozens of publishers have folded. That will not directly improve and the times of unbridled quantities of publishers in every field and theme will inevitably not come back. Innovative new publishers will undoubtedly arise to fill certain niches, but for the mainstream publisher there is no way back: they will have to choose one or more of the three publishing strategies.

I will describe the three types of publisher again independently starting with the self-publishing publisher.

I give clear proof that there will be not much room for many **self publishing publishers**. Regardless of the organizational effort (mediating for editors, type setters, marketers, etc.) and permanent IT investments and innovations, there will not be much room for many providers. Also because it is a service area, in principle, which is totally new to the current publishing industry.

Every self publishing publisher will be managed greatly on brand-theme combinations as a distinctive element to their customers; thereby virtually no room is left for the small, poorly funded, poorly profiled and badly organized parties.

However something should be added here: the branding of self publishing publishers will need to be strong in terms of publishing theme, because to the reader it should be immediately clear what he can find with the corresponding self-publisher. If that's not the case and if one only wants unlimited choice, then online stores like Amazon and Bol.com will stay big. Maybe a partnership between the publishers arises to set up such a department store environment or the CB will become a player. If it is well executed it may have a chance, but the window of opportunity is closing fast. And moreover it is another (consumer) game than the publishers are used to so far.

Also for the **middle publisher** - the form that most resembles the publisher as we know it - will have to aim strongly on theme and target audience. The big problem is that the reading public doesn't know the publisher, and the publisher has to leave behind his reflex of over-concentrating on content creation. This automatically means that this publisher will also have the hardest time. Richard D'Aveni called this phenomenon in his book *Hyper Competition* 'stuck in the middle'. Such publishers can hardly hold a dominant position, unless the game with the self-publishers on the one hand and the bestseller publishers on the other is well played: as a buyer of proven talent (of the self-publishers) and as a supplier of potential good selling authors (the bestseller publisher). It means there are still opportunities for dozens but not for hundreds of middle publishers.

The **bestseller publisher** will try to build a dominant position on certain themes. I think in the Dutch market there is room for a handful of bestseller publishers. The capital requirement and the deep pockets needed to set up a truly viable bestseller publisher will be substantial. The increasing budgets for advances of proven bestselling authors and titles support that thought.

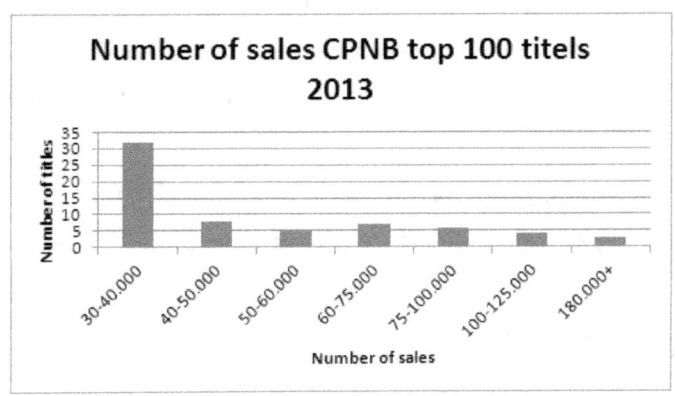

Fig. 16.2. Number of bestsellers in the Netherlands in 2013 (source: CPNB)

There are in the Netherlands - with the current pricing policy - a few hundred bestsellers per year (according to our definition approximately € 40,000 transfer price turnover or more). This has huge implications for the amount of bestseller publishers that the market can bear. If the pressure is high, the temptation will be great to set the limit for a bestseller lower than € 40,000, adopting old behavior. In my view, the challenge for the bestseller publisher is to stick to thinking big, to stick to big titles and not to be tempted to go for smaller ones. It will also be fascinating to see if the choice for a selection of themes will be held as consistently as possible.

To publish under the € 40,000 limit is of course possible, but it will be the domain of the middle publisher.

Margin

If we look at the profitability of the three strategic publisher types, it is striking that it is also about three different business models:

Self publishing publisher: a service publisher is mainly paid by the 'billing by the hour' principle. The reach among customers is exploitable and scalability is good: the more visitors and customers the better and reach will be monetised in one way or another with third parties. For example through advertising, but even more by exploiting profiles of readers. The billing by the hour, the service to authors, is less scalable: the more demand, the more staff, temporary staff and partners are necessary. There will also be more coordination necessary so that the margin for the publisher per activity does not increase.

5% is a good margin for this type of work, which is based on the volume of activities. In some cases, the margin will be zero or even negative. The publisher will fully focus to achieve maximum reach online and can make extra money by the transfer of potentially profitable authors to the middle publisher and bestseller publisher respectively.

The **middle publisher** would show better margins compared to the current average in the light of what we now know about 'publishing as we know it'. After all, there are fewer titles published and the amount of capital investment in non-performing titles is much lower than in the current situation. The middle publisher is typically a content creator with the associated business model, in which 10 to 15% should be a fair margin.

The **bestseller publishing house** is a capital-intensive industry where a 'winner takes all' business model makes sense; the implications to margins should be compared to the film industry: the great amount of money each title must deliver, will for the most part be spent beforehand, in advances in the form of the purchase of the manuscript and in huge marketing and distribution expenses.

What remains must be sufficient for the large budgets for the next round. The 'high risk, high return' principles are indeed never a guarantee of success (see the earlier chapter on the luck factor), but the idea behind it is that the most expensive title in costs this way generates more profit in absolute terms. Therefore an average of 15% profitability on the large sums we are talking about will be necessary to keep the expensive machine going.

Elberse states in her book that the profitability of the most expensive book in her example yielded about 35% profit (return on sales). Again at a bestseller publisher it is about the volume of money that is collected and the percentages are less important. Interesting to read with Elberse is her discussion of marketing costs per (blockbuster) film, which are relatively lower in very expensive movies than with less popular movies. On the one hand this is logical (the market can become saturated with too much advertising), on the other hand it reflects also the promotion effort to support additional advertising to an impending bad runner. Dividing the promotion budget will still have to be played intelligently.

Innovation budgets

The differences in character of the different publishers also become clear : The **self publishing publisher** will constantly have to compete and invest in functionality (for both authors and consumers) and in the big data sets that that entails, i.e. in ICT to let platforms operate as efficient and effective as possible. In addition, this publisher is a service provider par excellence and it will have to innovate in its processes and knwoledge. It will subsequently have to continue to invest in partnerships with suppliers (editing, distribution, cover art, etc.) and partners. Perhaps a small acquisition in its time. That is not cheap and quite capital intensive. Amazon invests year-on-year 6% of its turnover in its research and development. On average a publisher in the Netherlands currently does not invest more than 0.5% of its turnover per year. I believe that a rate of 5-10% of turnover is necessary and that immediately indicates why the current publishing industry is not profitable. The advantages of innovation arrive over time, but if one doesn't innovate they never arrive as explained earlier.

The **middle publisher** will have to spend its margins on marketing innovation, by developing knowledge about audiences and personas, to be able to purchase rights and innovate. They will have to invest in scouting authors (with the self-publishers) and author transfers (to the bestseller publishers). The capital intensity is not huge, so I think 5% will be sufficient.

The **bestseller publisher** will not start many autonomous innovations, as opposed to investments in the very effective use of distribution, promotion and marketing knowledge, and these investments it will continually keep up to date. Most innovation in this branch will consist of making acquisitions and collaborations. This may involve fellow (bestseller) publishers in other customer segments and investments in other topics than the own publishing house supports. Often also bestselling authors and backlists are bought at the same time. Therefore about 10% of sales per year will be required.

Chapter 17

Coherence and cooperation between the three types of publishing

In Appendix 1 I have outlined a structural basis for the above model. The relationship between the three publisher types is that the middle publisher and the bestselling publisher are better focused models than what usually has been the case, with self publishing being an obvious stepping stone to a different stage and a different approach to the role of the publisher and the author.

Interdependence

The coherence of the three forms is based on a model of cooperation and interdependence between these three forms:

If a successful author has been spotted in the self publishing environment (through existing middle publishers, agents or anyone else), the publisher may propose to transfer the copyright to the vicinity of a partner middle publisher. This operation is now at the expense and risk of the middle publisher but all parties now benefit from it:

. For the author, his success is a prelude to a better distribution of royalties, as he has proven himself in the meantime. For self published authors the hassle of self-promotion is a substantial effort and in the end it is still irresistible to be published by a publisher; because it also provides convenience in addition to status.

. The publisher of the middle publisher. has a risk lower than before: the author has already proven himself, often has a group of followers and can be better positioned with a targeted investment particularly in promotion and distribution. Marketing euros in short deliver more efficiency. However, it is clear that one divides the limited budget over a fixed number of titles. Formerly the dilution of the marketing budget on too many titles was at the expense of success.

. For the self publishing publisher there is a transfer fee or at least a financial mechanism for the delivery of a new talent.

The same principle also applies to transfers from middle to bestseller publisher: if the author also exceeds a certain threshold with sales and turnover then he can be transferred to the bestseller publisher. In the most negative case he must return to the self publishing environment.

The transfer fees that go with them, form part of the structure and business model per publisher type.

Combinations

Of course, the possibility is open to combine the three strategies under the umbrella of a single publishing house, and there may also be cooperation conglomerates of the three types of publishers.

Large publishing companies are able to pursue all three publishing strategies in multiple publishing themes but it is also possible to concentrate on one of the three forms, so long as the other two forms exist to co-operate with or to partner with. The knowledge and experience in the field of collaboration and partnering are a new competence for publishers and run as a common thread through this three tiered model. I'm not talking about cooperation on the basis of procurement groups, because these already exist. In this model it is about cooperation in many primary areas such as publishing rights and handling of rights, marketing and marketing intelligence, sales strategy and so on.

As a result innovation is a normal part of the conversation between the three types of collaborative publishing. After all, the desire to achieve maximum reach with an audience of readers on the one hand and a good supply of stories from authors on the other hand, should lead to an alignment between the publishers who want to score on the same theme. For new presentations, other distribution opportunities and to develop new -still unknown - environments one will need to work together.

There is also a caveat: it is absolutely not the intention to apply the three strategies within a smaller or medium-sized publisher, because one runs the risk of making the same mistake where it all started: no clear strategy and no focus.

[Test]

Consequences of new strategy types

It is obvious to test the publishers in the benchmark for verification of the new strategy types and explore what the consequences are.

I took for this purpose three publishers from the benchmark. These three publishing houses represent some archetypical publishers from the Dutch landscape: a loss-making and a profitable one and one in between profit and loss. These I have subjected to analysis and short 'what-if studies. We look at each publisher what the the consequences are

. if titles, sales and costs are replaced to selfpublishing;

. when the publisher becomes a middle publisher;

. if there is a possibility to be a best-seller publisher.

Chapter 18

The Loss Maker

Analysis

The benchmark defines publisher A as an example of a publisher who is in trouble on multiple fronts. The publisher produces about 500 titles a year and has a negative contribution of 12% compared to the total turnover. That means the overhead and the margin of the company cannot be offset. The publisher cannot support this for long, so strategic rethinking is in order here.

What are the causes and what strategy could publisher A follow? If we check the Benchmark clusters in the case of publisher A, we see the image below.

publisher A	titles	turnover	costs	margin
>60€	27	52%	31%	21%
40-60k€	24	14%	11%	3%
20-40k€	56	13%	19%	-6%
10-20k€	178	14%	34%	-20%
<10k€	217	7%	18%	-11%
total	502	100%	112%	-12%

Fig. 18.1 Publisher A - data per cluster related to total sales

The percentages are related to the total turnover for publisher A. What is immediately noticeable is that Publisher A performs poorly over the entire range of the turnover structure. Even the bestsellers (over € 40,000) did not perform well enough to compensate for the rest. The 502 titles issued cover a total of more than thirty NUR codes, so a clear thematic focus is not in place.

At a glance it becomes clear that more than half of the cost fall in the two smaller clusters up to € 20,000, which together account for over 30% of the negative contribution. The 27 major titles do have a contribution of 21% but they can not stop the leak at the bottom. It seems that the second square between € 10,000 and € 20,000 is doing the worst.

Looking further per cluster, three important elements turn out to do the damage:

Large manufacturing stocks. Approximately 50% of the cost is determined by the production of the books, and all loss-making clusters have a huge overproduction. The production costs, seen here compared to sales per cluster, are often a multiple thereof, as shown in the figure below. This illustrates the waste-debate once again: print runs are too optimistically planned causing a huge financial problem for the publisher.

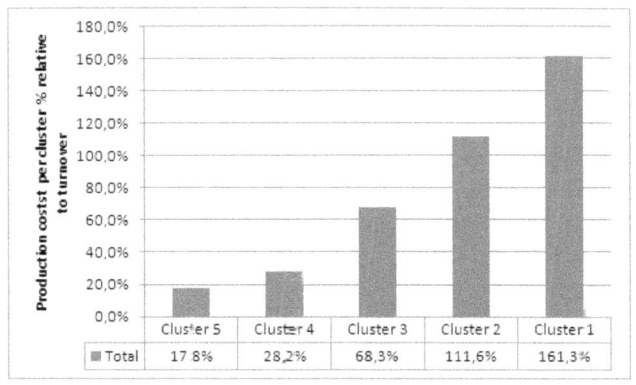

Fig. 18.2 Publisher A Productioncosts per cluster

Bad selling hardcovers. The analysis per cluster shows that the hardcovers sell badly and due to their higher costs are the main cause of disappointing results. As an example we show the titles, represented by beads, in the range from € 10,000 to € 20,000. First all the titles and then the hardcover titles.

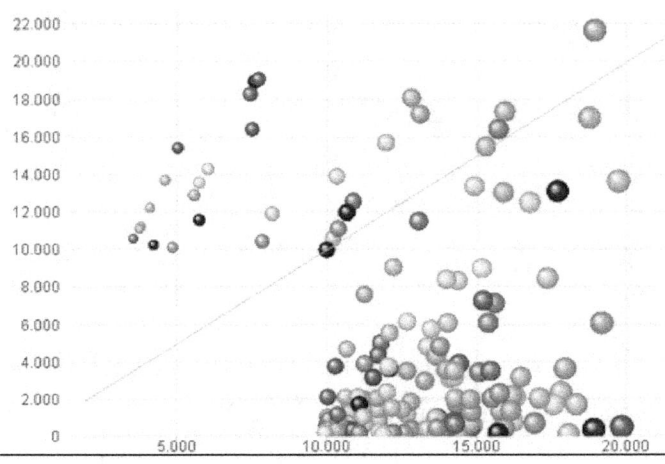

Fig. 18.3 Publisher A -Titles in Cluster 2 (€ 10.000 -€ 20.000) (Qlikview)

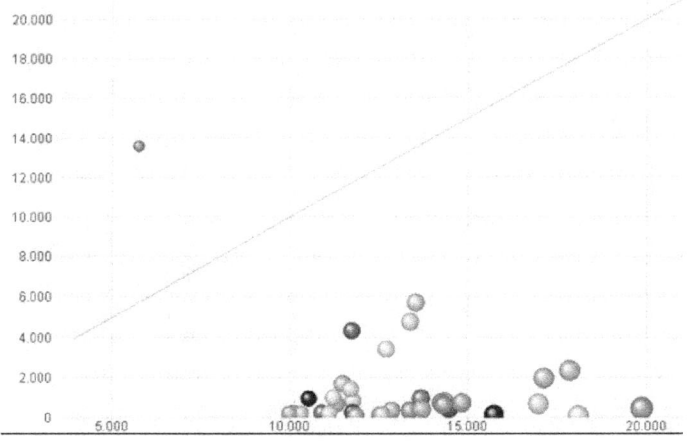

Fig. 18.4 Publisher A - Hardcover Titles in Cluster 2 (€10.000 - €20.000)
(Qlikview)

Translated foreign titles vs. Dutch titles. The publisher seems
to have an unfortunate hand in translated works and an unlucky
hand in producing Dutch-language manuscripts in the clusters with
the smallest sales. It is shown in the figure below.

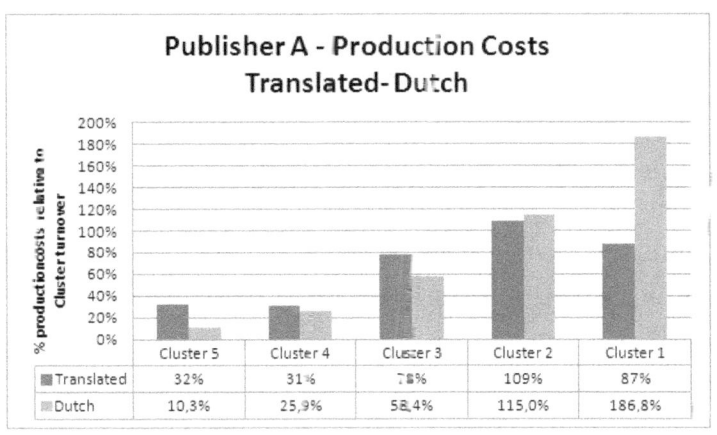

Figuur 18.5 Publisher A - production costs per type

Apart from the fact that there is still much more data to analyse the key question is what happens if this publisher is aiming for a different strategy. It seems there is no lack of energy and titles but a clear focus is missing with publisher A.

Strategic options

What would be the cure for this publisher? The first, most eye-catching point is the possible concentration on fewer themes. The provision of greater focus in this area will lead to more targeted decisions regarding choice of titles and investments therein.

Second, the print run policy should be scrutinized. There is too much produced for inventory which has not been sold. Internally simple agreements are needed on limiting print runs and, if necessary, POD solutions or just-in-time methods as discussed in Chapter 6.

If we extend this to a possible strategy: which form or forms of strategy would be eligible for this publisher? Let's walk them through:

Self Publishing Publisher. The number of titles that are produced in Dutch at the bottom clusters may show this publisher is trying to cultivate new talent. Practically, it proves to be a heavy financial burden, so it would be wise to accommodate those very activities in a self-publishing publisher, where the attention and the risk is borne by the authors rather than the publisher. This also applies to foreign translated works, which are pursued by this publisher at much effort and cost, but with no great successes in return.

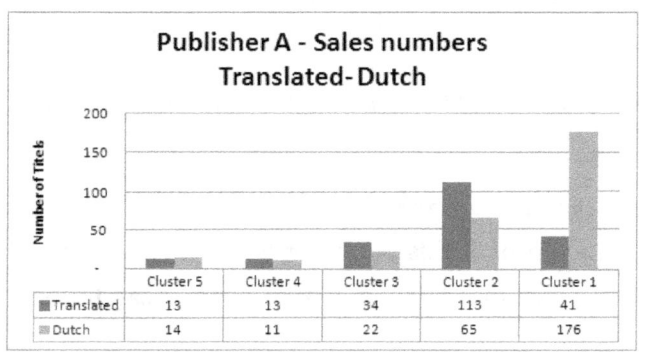

Fig. 18.6 Numbers of translated foreign titles and Dutch titles

Middle publisher. Is this publisher an outstanding mid publisher, then? I think so. If one gets the production discipline in order, with about 25-30% improvement, there is a basis for a healthy operation in the clusters between € 10,000 and € 40,000. This also means that there is a substantial farewell to large purchases of foreign works, because they provide a disproportionately poor contribution to the bottom line. If everything below the € 10k mark is removed, the Dutch titles alone are obviously profitable. That is about an odd 90 Dutch titles and a handful of foreign translated works.

Bestseller publisher. Is this not also a bestseller publisher? After all, there are in total 50 titles that do particularly well in turnover and margin.

If there is also extra focus in terms of cost control these titles might show even better results. The database shows that with this publisher it handles mainly about titles which have an average age of between 1 and 2 years. That in itself is not a bad starting point for a bestseller publisher. However, it remains to be seen whether the pockets are deep enough to acquire and to promote successful bestsellers and thus make the bestseller publisher grow.

Publisher A faces a number of fundamental choices: the divestment of activities and titles into a self-publishing publisher and at the same time finding a way how to cooperate with that same selfpublishing publisher to continue to 'breed' aspiring authors. And in addition, it is also important to make the choice between the restructuring of its middle publisher activities on the one hand, and whether or not to continue with a bestseller activity on the other. All three together has clearly not worked and will mean the demise of the publisher. But the options and analyses to make informed choices are at least at hand.

Chapter 19

The Profit Maker

Analysis

Publisher D seems to be an example of a successful publisher. We will examine where it stems from. The figures show that the 260 titles that have been made in the recent period have led to a contribution of 38% of turnover. It seems that most efforts into bestsellers itself pays off handsomely: the said contribution of 38% of turnover with nearly two thirds of all costs is related to titles above € 60,000. However, even more interestingly a large number of titles in the two lower clusters (more than half of the total number of titles) yield a negative contribution. So it is not all peace and harmony.

publisher D	titles	turnover	costs	margin
>60€	46	77%	39%	38%
40-60k€	19	8%	5%	3%
20-40k€	42	9%	8%	1%
10-20k€	57	4%	6%	-2%
<10k€	96	2%	4%	-2%
total	260	100%	62%	38%

Figuur 19.1 Publisher D data per cluster related to total sales

The number of NUR codes publisher D covers amount to 10, of which three consist of only one title. So it seems there is a good focus on theme and subject area. What is intriguing is the loss-making activities at the lower clusters and particularly the amount of effort that must be performed there. It is about 10% of the total cost if we talk about titles up to € 20,000 and 18% up to € 40,000. But the bulk of the titles - nearly 200 pieces - are in those segments.

Compared to Publisher A this seems well managed, so the first reaction is: what a waste. It would seem that we are dealing with a bestseller publisher. Why would a bestseller publisher produce so many other, smaller titles? First we'll take a look in more detail at the costs.

Production costs. Production costs measured in relation to turnover in the relevant cluster are listed below. They seem excellent at first glance (and well within the benchmark of the entire population of publishers), particularly in the clusters of lower sales where it usually goes wrong. It looks like this publisher manages his print runs and inventory well. But the amount of effort and attention it takes to produce everything between 100 and 200 titles at the lower clusters and to promote and sell them seems an unnecessary fragmentation for a bestseller publisher and thus: waste. The figure indicates the percentage of production costs compared to sales in the same cluster.

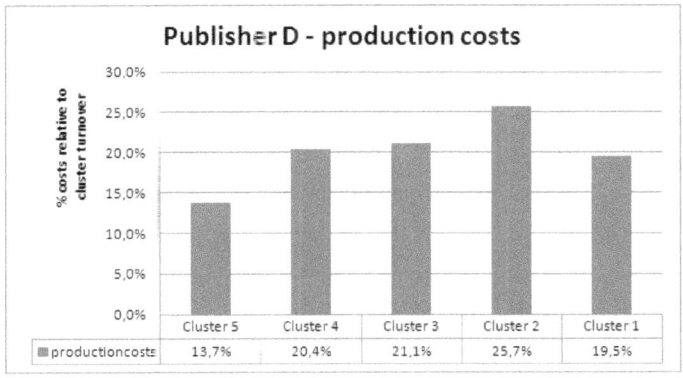

Figuur 19.2 Publisher D Production costs per cluster

In production terms, we can not actually accuse this publisher of creating waste. The product form (paperback, hardcover, etc.) is not a cause for worry, either.

Translated, non-translated. Upon closer examination, it is particularly the cost of translation and layout costs which drag the smaller titles down. That is not surprising considering that translation costs are always directly felt in small editions and in this case also relative to small turnovers. All inevitable costs such as editing and translation costs weigh heavily in the end result, and that is the case here.

There will undoubtedly have been cuts in promotion costs which otherwise would continue to have negative influence on the result. And in a nutshell the dilemma unfolds for the bottom clusters of this publisher: one can be as tough as possible on production costs, but if the title is not promoted in the right way in the market, it remains a minor title.

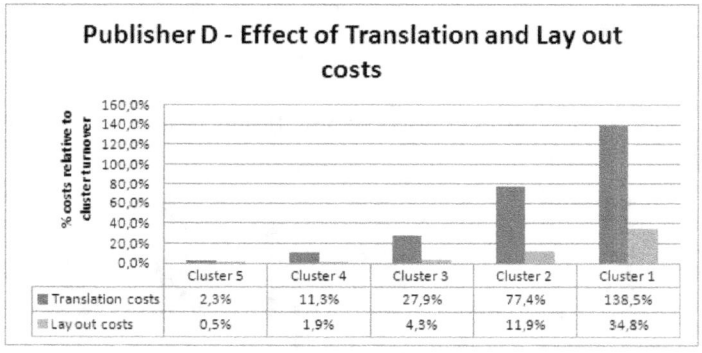

Fig. 19.3 Publisher D Effect of translation and layout costs

As for focus it is clear that this publisher purchases foreign titles in a controlled manner. In all clusters the foreign titles dominate, sometimes to an extreme degree, except under € 10,000, where the Dutch authors are the majority.

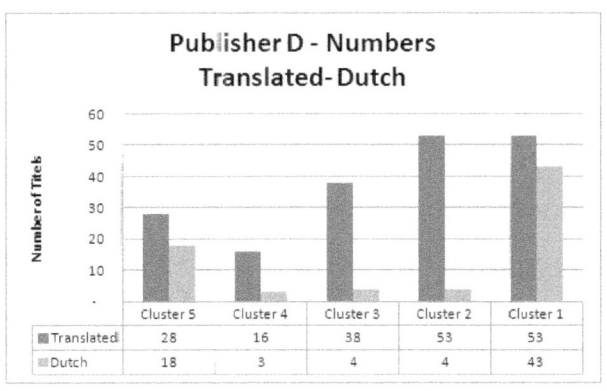

Fig. 19.4 Publisher D Numbers of titles translated, not translated (Dutch).

Strategic options

Publisher D seems to have everything: focus on the theme, focus on where they purchase texts and rights, solid income, firm cost control. What are the strategic options here?

With this publisher sharpening the focus and making more space to grow would be the obvious way to go. Sharpening the focus should be to strategically look at what is happening with authors and titles at the bottom clusters. That means even more daring a focus: the courage to initiate genuine major titles and no to put energy at the bottom clusters is obviously scary but the consequence. Further growth in the existing target group and theme combination, for example through acquisitions on the same theme, or by developing new audiences for that theme. The winner takes all strategy should be the way to go here.

> **Self Publisher.** It is important to decide that the current bottom clusters of publisher D are awarded to a different environment. That could be a self publishing environment in which publisher D participates or with which it cooperates to identify potential (bestseller) talent.

Both people and resources thus released can be used to create more successful bestsellers, as we have suggested in previous chapters. Also one could invest in participating with innovative companies that will connect to target audiences in a different way than the bestselling publisher could do on its own.

Middle publisher. Collaborations with middle publishers with the aim of agreements on the acquisition and exploitation of potential best sellers is the most likely scenario. Maybe the further professionalisation of the procurement of foreign manuscripts belongs here too. Successful titles are already available, it seems, but there must always be room for more.

On paper publisher D is a good example of a bestseller publisher who can still develop further. Daring to choose for focus and the 'winner-takes-all strategy' are no easy tasks, and they require many adjustments in deployment of people and resources. But the basis for this exists and looks healthy.

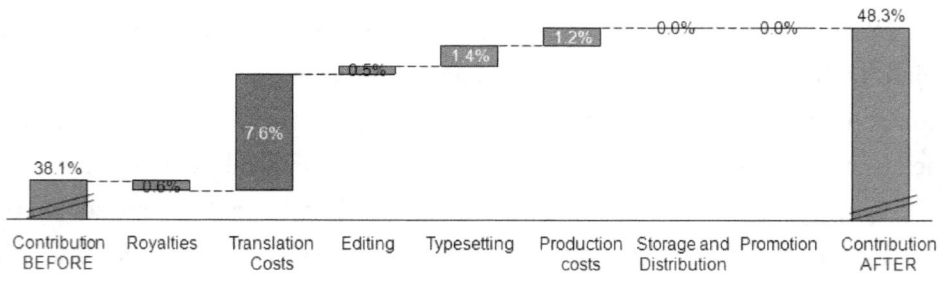

Fig. 19.5 Margin percentage improvement in Publisher D by focusing on bestseller publisher

Figure 19.5 shows what the improvements are if publisher D chooses to position itself as a bestseller publisher. It reveals what happens if and when it deliberately leaves the clusters 1, 2 and 3 and what improvements will result from it. Especially improvements by reducing translation costs (because those titles will not be created anymore) stand out

Chapter 20

The Mainstream publisher

Analysis

At first glance for Publisher G a lot has to be done on strategy. The publisher shows the symptoms that more publishers experience: there are too few bestsellers to appropriately subsidize the smaller titles internally. The 179 titles produced have a kind of iceberg structure: a small tip protrudes just above it. However, a large part is literally under water, as a contribution of 1 and 3 percent respectively is a de facto loss-making operation.

publisher G	titles	turnover	costs	margin
>60€	9	58%	28%	30%
40-60k€	5	7%	5%	3%
20-40k€	20	15%	14%	1%
10-20k€	56	14%	23%	-10%
<10k€	89	7%	15%	-9%
total	179	100%	86%	14%

Fig. 20.1 Publisher G - data per cluster related to total sales

NUR codes. Zooming in on the causes and effects there is a remarkable fragmentation on the themes. There are investments on twenty NUR codes, whereby four themes really stand out, but there is also published on various other topics. What are the consequences if we look at the figures?

Of those NUR codes contributions in all clusters are expressed in the Figure below. By NUR code one can see if there is a positive contribution or not. For many of the NUR codes where little is spent on opportunism is not rewarded. But also a few NUR codes which do contain several titles have a negative contribution. A discussion focusing on themes is necessary here.

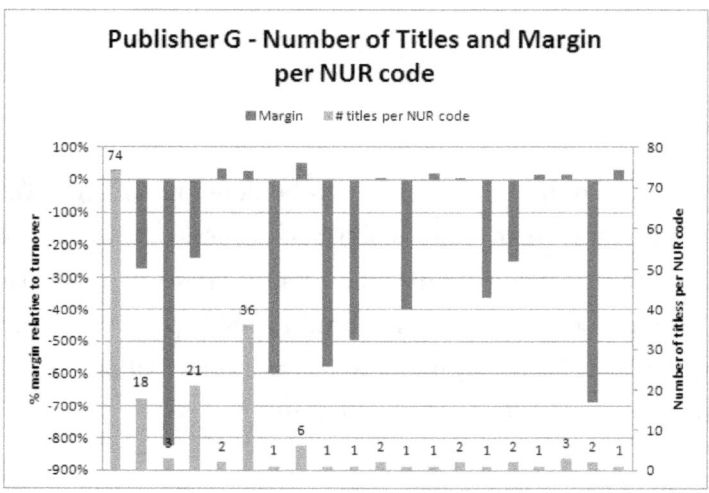

Fig. 20.2 Publisher G - Number of titles and contributions by NUR code

Production costs. Also with this publisher production costs are a recurring theme. The division in translated titles and Dutch origin titles is skewed which may have to do with the themes and subjects that the publisher has chosen. The figures also show that improvemenst can made on print runs and editions.

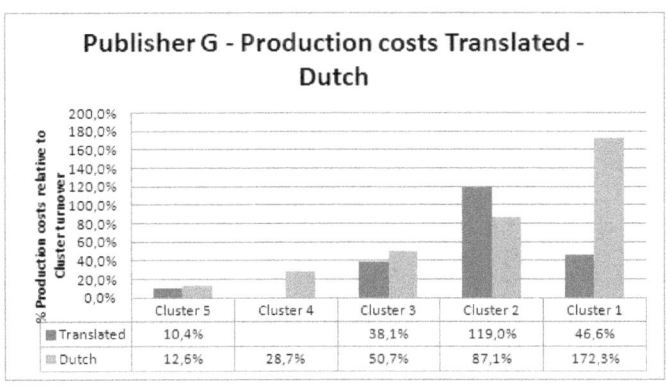

Fig. 20.3 Publisher G - production costs per translated / Dutch title.

Strategic options

Publisher G has a problem: to choose. It is not a bestseller publisher, at least not yet. The publisher looks more like a middle publisher, but then the themes will have to be adjusted. Firmly choosing seems appropriate here, especially on themes. From there a choice for the kind of publisher will be easier to make.

> **Self Publishing**. The titles at the bottom clusters of this publisher deserve a better fate, and self-publishing should be considered. For the publisher himself the image below is revealing enough. For a dozen titles that are above the line all cost elements should be scrutinised and decided whether they are viable titles. And whether they match the theme one chose to focus on.

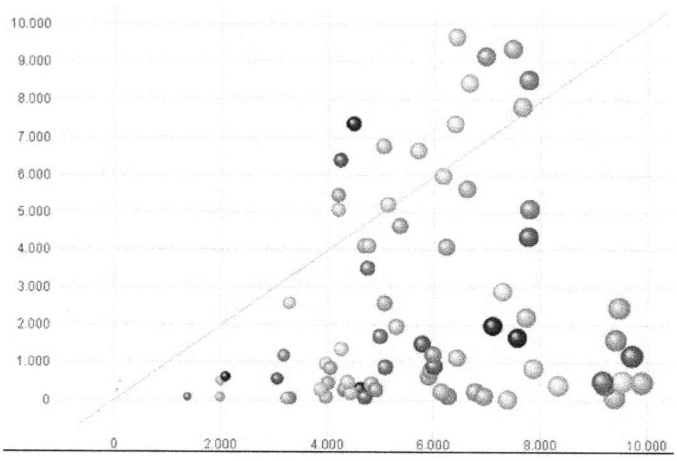

Fig. 20.4 Publisher G - Cluster 1 (Qlikview)

Middle publisher. If we detach in the figures the self-publishing cluster 1, a company remains with a positive 28% contribution. But if we also take away the bestsellers-clusters 4 and 5, there remains minus 32%.

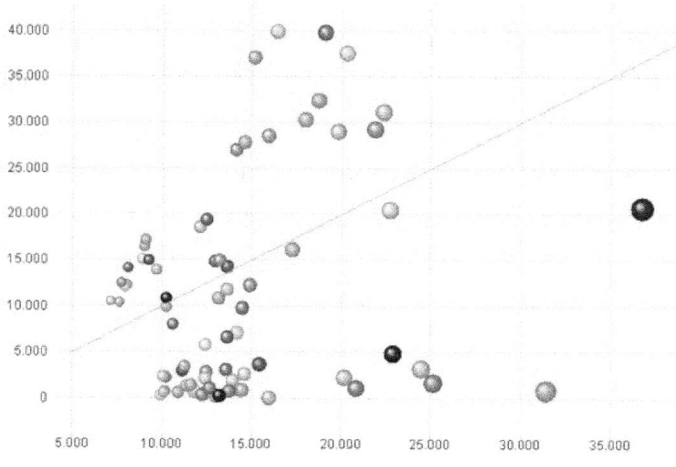

Fig. 20.5 Publisher G - titles between € 10,000 and € 40,000 (Qlikview)

The task at hand is to assess the titles below the line on theme and costs. Production costs appear to be high, so there is still a lot to gain. A small calculation provides that with a focus on four NUR-codes the contribution was exactly zero. After that production costs were reduced, yielding a 25% end result. Sales fell with all these actions by 17%. The conclusion is that this publishing house can be tuned into a middle publisher if and only if there is a focus on both theme and print runs.

Bestseller Publisher. Is there a possibility for label G to become a bestseller publisher? In theory with 14 titles divided over five themes that is no easy task, but the real problem is that currently 40 percent of the turnover is determined by a single title. In short, there is no spread of risk. And the large budgets needed for the acquisition of a number of its successors are limited. It would be a very high risk / high return strategy to choose for becoming a bestseller publisher

It will require enormous discipline for this publisher to free himself from the current happy go lucky way of publishing to becoming a focused publisher. As said, this is the general problem most publishers face. There are indeed strategic options that differ in approach, but again a choice for a clear solution will certainly lead to a final farewell to waste and decline.

[Epilogue]

The motivation for writing this book is my surprise about the waste in the publishing industry and the way how it is handled. The analyses that I have given in this book should serve as a wake-up call: if we continue in the present way, sooner or later the last publisher will have to turn off the light. An industry that does not seem to be able to save something as beautiful as 'the narrative experience through reading' should be helped by daring to look differently at itself.

I have proposed a new model for publishing. The idea with this model is to diminish the waste in the supply chain and to advocate a healthy financing of the publishing industr. The locked up money in a variety of unsaleable books at the bottom of the market is thus avoided. There will be more money to spend on attracting readers in the direction of selected titles they really want and need.

Moreover with the model it is possible to invest more money in finding out the needs of the reader or those of the distribution channel or the author. In other words, there is more budget left for further development and innovation of the market.

Also, a gain of the model is its focus on certain parts of the market. Where currently all kinds of topics and target groups are served within a single publishing company, this transition brings along much more focus and thus develops useful skills within the industry on themes and marketing.

With the new insights and strategies I have presented, I hope new impetus is regained within the publishing industry. I also expect that new entrants to the market can benefit with these insights and strategies. So a new generation of entrepreneurs can start to bring the 'narrative experience' in an innovative manner to a large, new and interested audience.

Hermann Buss, january 2016

[Annex A]

Context for the chosen strategy

In *The granularity of growth* of Patrick Viguerie c.s. a practical growth map is unfolded along which strategically the growth of an industry can be drawn. Using the growth chart below the strategy proposed by me has been substantitated.

Briefly Viguerie indicates that there are basically three strategic options (cylinders) for growing in revenue and profitability :

.organic growth through focus and innovation

.growth through acquisitions (and / or through the divestment of activities)

.growth by expanding market share

At first sight this is not particularly revolutionary, but because Viguerie has built a database of hundreds of companies conclusions are drawn about which combinations of these three strategies can work best.

For publishers, I did an estimate based on the current state of affairs for the market in the Netherlands (see details in Chapter 1). The average growth rate during the period of 2009-2014 (called Compound Aggregate Growth Rate or CAGR) was 4.4% per annum for P-books and E-books combined.

The estimated breakdown of the three growth components are outlined below, which shows that less was extracted from the products themselves (organic growth) and at the same time it lost market share overall. With sales and divestitures some turnover and profitability was compensated for.

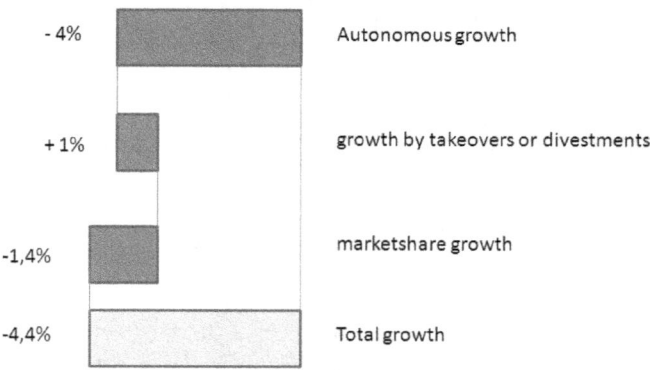

Fig. A1. Distribution CAGR-publishing industry Netherlands in growth cylinders
(source : expert view)

This illustrates once again the earlier message that the market is declining overall, but the question is this: what can you do to turn these three cylinders into a successful combination?

If you look at the cylinders even further for the most interesting combinations in the future, then a nice framework emerges from which one can evaluate one's strategy. Viguerie defines three horizons that lie further away in time. First time horizon is to defend and expand the existing business, the next step assumes that you will continue to develop emerging products and the third phase should provide more forward-looking growth options. All the steps you are going to do for that growth need time and vary by industry and also by each individual company.

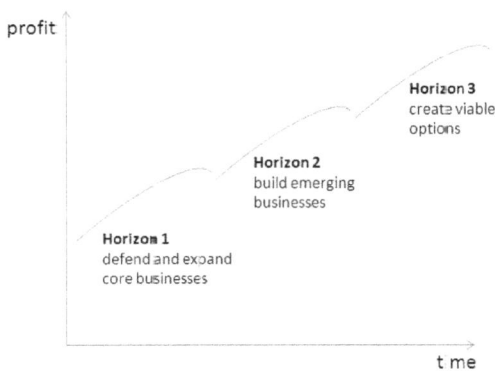

Figuur A2. The three growth horizons, source Viguerie et al.

The three horizons in particular introduce a line in business development, so that there can be a lasting and profitable growth.It is - as highlighted by Viguerie - a way to create a structure for the direction in which you can change. And it gives possibilities to define actions that you can use as an industry or (in the individual case) as a company. The connection Viguerie makes between the three strategic cylinders and the three time phases leads to a growth chart, within which one can make all kinds of choices.

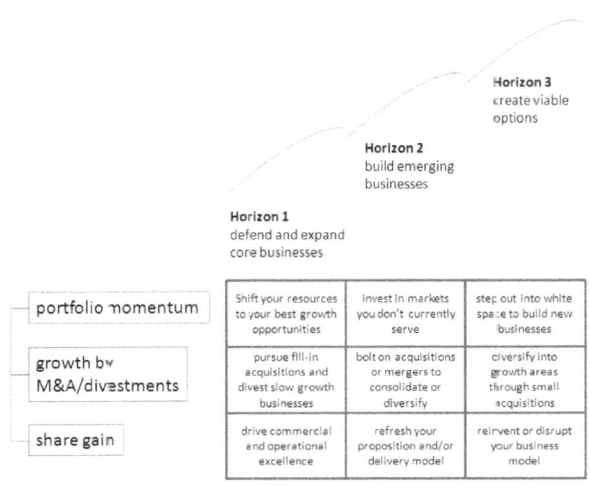

Fig. A 3. Growth Cylinders, source Viguerie et al.

What makes it interesting is that the current strategy in book publishing has mainly focused on the cylinder 'growth by taking over and divesting'. 'Organic growth' or 'autonomous portfolio momentum' by bringing more focus (eg focus on theme) has been adopted in recent years by only a few publishers. 'Market Share Increase' or 'share gain' by reducing costs, also known as operational excellence, has been applied by publishers mainly by cutting production costs, for example by trying to put printers under pressure to deliver lower prices. But hardly not by process standardization, such as book form standardization and format standardization.

The above decisions have barely resulted in a different approach to the creative and editorial process, where also much can be improved. Additional sales opportunities, also called Commercial excellence, has been deployed on several fronts, but the demise of Polare in the Netherlands and the crisis in the bookstore itself did not help much here. Truly innovative growth initiatives in commercial terms, for example through new distribution tactics, have not really got off the ground.

All this leads to the following picture of the strategy which the industry currently - in general - has adopted. As can be seen in Figure A4 on the one hand mainly by divesting or just by consolidating with a focus on medium-term results and on the other hand by some rationalising (cost savings) in the short term. Again, the publishing industry lacks strong long-term initiatives.

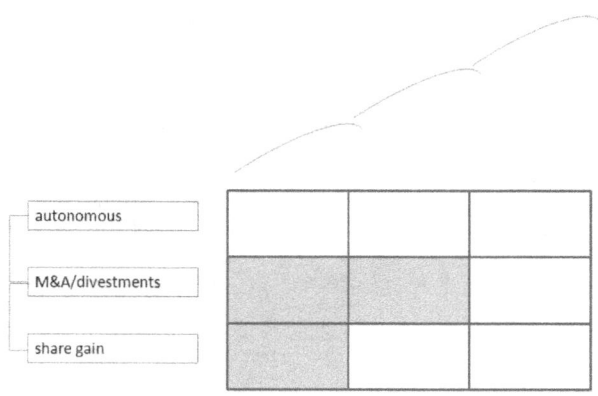

Fig. A4. Projection current growth strategy publishers

Horizon 2 initiatives are taken reluctantly with websites where direct selling takes place, but de facto Amazon and Bol.com have taken a large slice of the business already.The cylinder 'autonomous' for example, contains streaming applications, including initiatives of VBK and long announced initiatives by Lannoo and WPG. It is a pity that new initiatives are often left to the market, where giants like Amazon and Bol.com are active. Of course the important point is self publishing, which we have given much attention in this book. Figure A5 plots the existing growth strategy complemented by these fledgling initiatives of publishers.

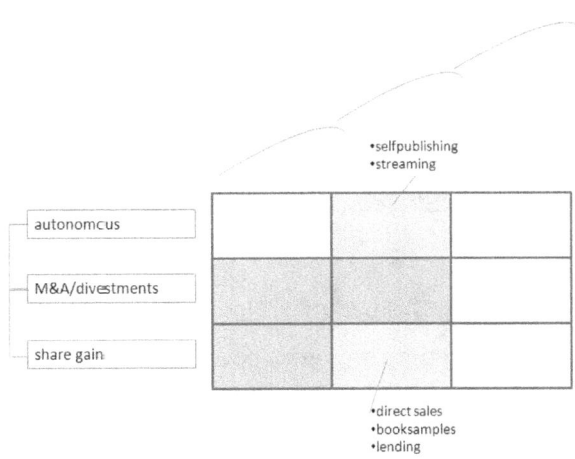

Fig. A5. projected growth strategy publishers supplemented by competitive initiatives

The strategy of Bestsellers and Badsellers we advocate in this book can be easily visualized by the growth map :

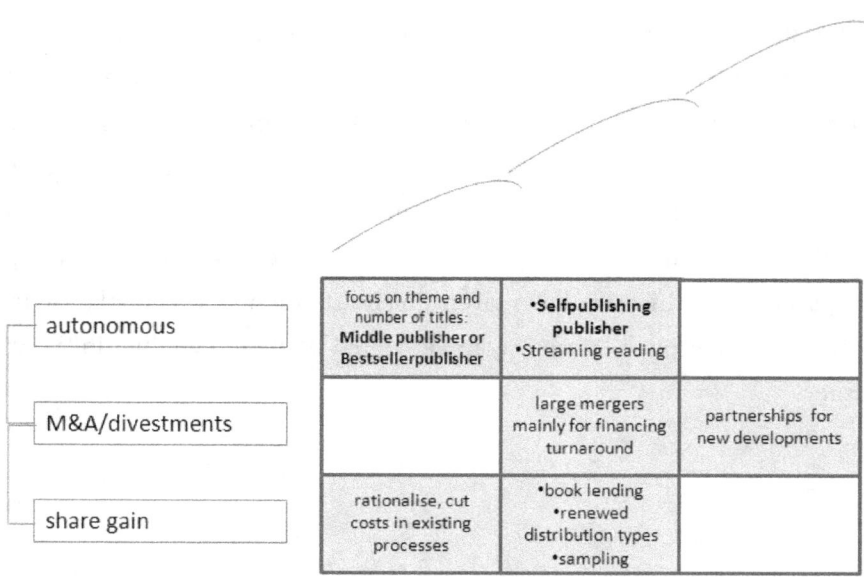

	focus on theme and number of titles: **Middle publisher or Bestsellerpublisher**	•**Selfpublishing publisher** •Streaming reading	
autonomous			
M&A/divestments		large mergers mainly for financing turnaround	partnerships for new developments
share gain	rationalise, cut costs in existing processes	•book lending •renewed distribution types •sampling	

Fig. A6. Strategy Bestsellers en Badsellers

This representation indicates that the strategy works on all different cylinders and that there is a time sequence possible. The time sequence, however, strongly depends on the company and the marketsegment in which the publisher operates. It is my conviction that the three time horizons already very closely overlap.

Streaming is already an existing solution, just as (digital) lending and the models that are adopted for those initiatives. In short, quick action is needed and that is precisely why this book was written. What this picture also shows is that efforts will be made simultaneously in many areas. That's not a foregone conclusion because, for example, it will not always be financially feasible or required skills are lacking. It is important to come up with some intermediate strategies, such as starting only a bestseller publisher or just to fall back to the middle publisher or in establishing strong collaborations with parties operating in the other cylinders.

Other publishing branches

For comparison, I outline here the visualizations from other publishing sectors. These are generalizations of the Dutch market. The differences between the publishing sectors are large, where in particular the science publishers and the publishers for professionals are operating (strategically) smart. The other sectors of the publishing industry are struggling. On the one hand they are mainly trying to absorb the decline in the market within their companies and on the other hand they are seriously hindered due to lack of profitability and the lack of associated capital.

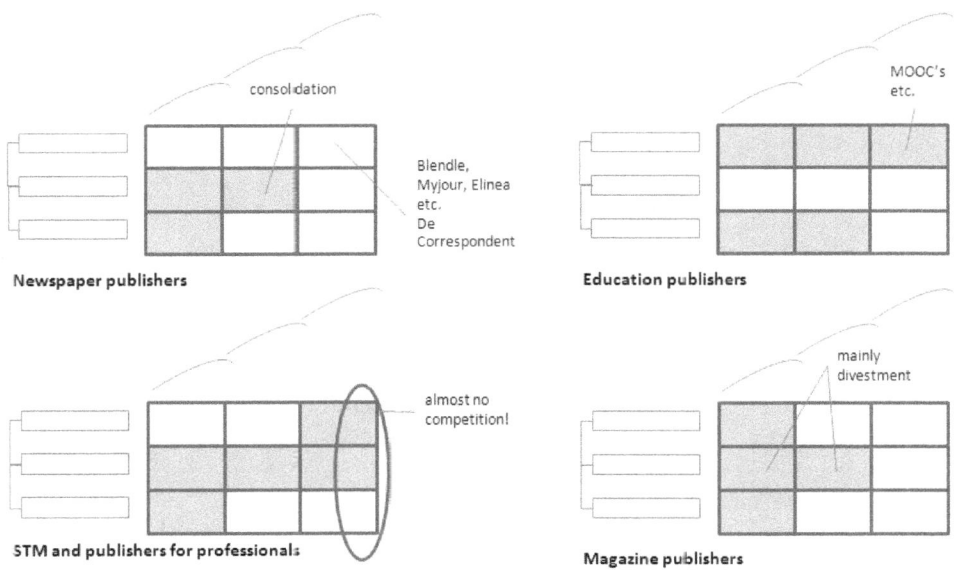

Fig. A7 Projection growth strategy of other publishing branches

[Annex B]

Benchmark elements

The benchmark has been set up on the basis of data per published ISBN. Per ISBN a.o. the following elements were gathered, the elements in bold being the minimum data provided by publishers:

a   Retail price (ex. VAT)
b   **Numbers sold (18 months cumulative)**
c   Turnover
d   # pages
e   **Print format**
f   **Numbers printed**
g   Royalties
h   Editing
i   Lay out/typesetting
j   E-book
k   **Print costs per book numbers sold**
l   **Storage and distribution costs**
m   **Promotion**
n   Overhead
o   Total costs (P- book)
p   Total costs (E-book)
q   **NUR-code**
r   **Dutch/Translated**
s   **Date first appearance**

Fig. B1 Elements Benchmark Bestsellers and Badsellers

[Recommended and used literature]

auteur	titel	
Andersen, Chris	Free, The future of a radical price	2009
Andersen, Chris	The Long Tail, How endless choice is creating unlimited demand	2006
Ashok et al.	Success with Style: Using Writing Style to Predict the Success of Novels; *Proceedings of the 2013 Conference on Empirical Methods in Natural Language Processing*	2013
Clark, Giles	Inside Book Publishing	1988 e.v.
d'Aveni, Richard	Hypercompetition, Managing the dynamics of strategic maneuvering	1994
d'Aveni, Richard	Strategic Supremacy	2001
Deloitte	Technology, Media, telecommunication predictions 2015	2014
Dosdoce.com	How to collaborate with startups, *research report*	2013
Elberse, Anita	Blockbusters , Hit-making, risk-taking, and the big business of entertainment	2013
Matheson, Jim and David	The Smart Organisation, Creating value through strategic R&D	1998
McIlroy, Thad	Venture Funding in the Bookpublishing Industry, *presentatie Slideshare*	2014
Murphy, James S.	When will machines start predicting bestsellers, Blogpost theawl.com	2014
Thompson, John B.	Merchants of Culture, The publishing business in the 21st century	2012
Viguerie et al.	The Granularity of Growth, Making choices that drive enduring company performance	2007

[Useful Links]

Deloitte - *Technology, Media, Telecommunication predictions 2015* - http://www2.deloitte.com/global/en/pages/technology-media-and-telecommunications/articles/tmt-predictions.html

Thad Mc Ilroy - *Venture funding in the Bookpublishing Industry* - http://www.slideshare.net/thadmc/venture-funding

Dosdoce *How to collaborate with start-ups,* http://www.dosdoce.com/articulo/estudios/3815/how-to-collaborate-with-startups/3815/how-to-collaborate-with-startups/

Amazon and Hachette - *article series Guardian* - http://www.theguardian.com/books/2014/nov/13/amazon-hachette-end-dispute-E-books

ALCS - *What are words worth now* - http://www.alcs.co.uk/CMSPages/GetFile.aspx?nodeguid=bd0b3ae5-759e-4d9e-81d5-06c406c68ee6

Jasper Henderson - *Een hopeloze spagaat. Over de (vermeende) ondergang van de redacteur* - http://www.groene.nl/artikel/een-hopeloze-spagaat (Dutch)

Tarifs of the Centraal Boekhuis - http://www.cb-logistics.nl/wp-content/uploads/2014/02/Compacte-dienstverlening-voor-uitgeverijen2014.pdf

NOM http://www.nommedia.nl/

Motivaction - http://www.motivaction.nl/mentality/het-mentality-model

Ashok et al. *Success with style* - http://sb.cc.stonybrook.edu/news/general/01062014CHOI.php

James S. Murphy - http://www.theawl.com/2014/01/when-will-the-machines-start-predicting-bestsellers

Book Lamp - http://techcrunch.com/2014/07/25/applE-booklamp/

NUR codes - http //www.boek.nl/nur

Random   House   Customer   Insights   Team   -
http://authornews.penguinrandomhouse.com/random-house-builds-consumer-insight-capabilities/#more-2847

[Finally]

A word of thanks to all persons who have contributed to the creation of this book. All conversations over the years with publishers, production staff, software geeks, editors, marketers and commercial staff. There are too many to mention but I especially want to thank the following people: my colleagues at GEA consultancy Michiel Klein and Patrick Swart and Karlijn Meijer, Tommy Heijnis and Erik Clabbers; the huge financial and modeling discussions and the struggle with our partners of Finext, Maarten Bronda and Nikita Maniram; the substantial involvement of Petra Rijkelijkhuizen. And the unwavering support of my wife Jeannette, who is still cool about all my stories about bestsellers and badsellers.

[About the Author]

'A friend is someone who knows everything about you and still loves you'.

Augustinus

Hermann Buss is an experienced manager, consultant and entrepreneur at the cutting edge of publishing and high-tech applications. He has built his career in various small and large companies in the Netherlands and abroad and has held management and executive positions at Philips Electronics, KPN and Wolters Kluwer. He works for clients in business, government, education and not-for-profit. He is the founder of Publishing Portfolio, a platform for change in publishing and an environment for education. Hermann studied electrical engineering, information theory and telecommunications at the Technical University Delft and became proficient in strategy at London Business School.

www.ingramcontent.com/pod-product-compliance
Lightning Source LLC
Chambersburg PA
CBHW070245190526
45169CB00001B/307